Praise for *BIFF for Lawyers and Law Offices*

"BIFF is simple, powerful, and impactful. This book should be mandatory reading for the entire legal industry. Once you start to use BIFF, it becomes an antidote for caustic interactions. You can't stop the poison, but BIFF gives you an antidote to counteract it safely. Read it, apply it, and start to use power of BIFF."

> — Attorney STEVE RILEY, Atticus Advantage – attorney coaching and law firm management training, and host of *Great Practice, Great Life* podcast

"The genius of Bill Eddy and his BIFF response method for lawyers and law offices is to make that potentially complicated world simple and straightforward. A brilliant, easy-to-remember tool in a lawyer's toolkit, *BIFF for Lawyers and Law Offices* has the potential to change the legal landscape by reducing conflict, crafting compromise, and focussing on solutions. BIFF has the power to transform a lawyer's life - I only wish I had discovered it sooner!

In short:

> **BRIEF**, bottom line — I use BIFF and it works!
>
> **INFORMATIVE**, reducing the potential for conflict by using facts rather than threats.
>
> **FRIENDLY** lawyers — who knew! Dispelling the myth that having an aggressive lawyer is a benefit to their clients, their staff, and the justice system as a whole.
>
> **FIRM** approach by being clear, efficient, and kind in communication, providing swifter negotiation and more cost-effective justice."

> —ELAINE E RICHARDSON, UK family solicitor, mediator, supervisor and trainer

"BIFF is an essential communication tool for all legal professionals. Bill Eddy and Rehana Jamal empower us to quickly and confidently respond to toxic communication and high-conflict people. Packed with useful examples, this book helps you calmly navigate stressful situations and make you more productive."

— MICHAEL J. LOMAX, JD, co-author of
Mediating High-Conflict Disputes

"As a family law attorney, mediator, and divorce podcaster, I can confidently say that *BIFF for Lawyers and Law Offices* is an invaluable resource. I still remember finding Bill's books when I was a young attorney and being so grateful for the strategies and insights he shared. I have implemented his management techniques ever since. This new book equips legal professionals with a practical and ethical approach to handling hostile communications, a skill that is indispensable in our field. The BIFF method's emphasis on brevity, informativeness, friendliness, and firmness is a game-changer, not only for lawyers but also for anyone dealing with conflict in their work."

— SUSAN GUTHRIE, leading family law attorney and
host of *The Divorce & Beyond* podcast

"Bill Eddy, along with co-author, Rehana Jamal, have produced another outstanding BIFF book - this one written for lawyers and law offices. The 10 BIFF questions reduce conflict and inspire productive communication. BIFF can be used by anyone."

—RHONDA LEE RUDMAN, Attorney at Law

BIFF

FOR LAWYERS AND LAW OFFICES

BIFF

FOR LAWYERS AND LAW OFFICES

YOUR GUIDE TO RESPECTFUL WRITTEN COMMUNICATION WITH CLIENTS, OPPOSING COUNSEL AND OTHERS

BILL EDDY, LCSW, ESQ.
REHANA JAMAL, JD, LL.M.

UNHOOKED BOOKS
Independent Publishers since 2011
an imprint of High Conflict Institute Press
Scottsdale, Arizona

Publisher's Note

Printed in the United States of America
First Edition
For information about permission to reproduce selections from this book, write to info@unhookedbooks.com or use the Contact Form at www.unhookedbooks.com.

Cover design by Julian León, The Missive
Interior Design by Jeffrey Fuller, Shelfish

ISBN (print): 9781950057399
ISBN (ebook): 9781950057405
Library of Congress Control Number: 2023947533

Unhooked Media, 7701 E. Indian School Rd., Ste. F, Scottsdale, AZ 85251
www.unhookedmedia.com

The publisher wishes to thank Jess Beebe for the fine editing of this book, and a special thank you to Nadia Weinmann for the Venn diagram on page 15 and helping with final proofing.

Also by Bill Eddy

Conflict Communication Series:
  BIFF: Quick Responses to High Conflict People, Their Personal Attacks and Social Media Meltdowns
  BIFF for Co-Parent Communication
  BIFF at Work
  Calming Upset People with EAR

Mediating High Conflict Disputes
High Conflict People in Legal Disputes
Managing High Conflict People in Court
The Future of Family Court
It's All Your Fault at Work! Managing Narcissists and other High-Conflict People
5 Types of People Who Can Ruin Your Life
Why We Elect Narcissists & Sociopaths—and How We Can Stop
Dating Radar
So, What's Your Proposal
It's All Your Fault! 12 Tips for Managing People Who Blame Others for Everything
Don't Alienate the Kids! Raising Resilient Children While Avoiding High Conflict Divorce
Splitting: Protecting Yourself While Divorcing Someone with Borderline or Narcissistic Personality Disorder
Splitting America

New Ways for Families in Separation and Divorce:
  Professional Guidebook
  Parent Workbook
  Collaborative Parent Workbook
  Decision Skills Class Instructor's Manual & Workbook
  Pre-Mediation Coaching Manual & Workbook
  Online Course Coaching Manual

New Ways for Work Coaching Manual & Workbook

New Ways for Life Instructor Guide & Youth Journal

*To my wife Alice, who always encouraged me to
persevere in the ups and downs of law practice, and to
make a positive difference in people's lives.*

—Bill

*To my family, who always supported my passions,
encouraged me to pursue a career in conflict resolution,
and understood my desire to make an impact
on people's lives.*

—Rehana

Contents

Introduction

This book provides a simple and proven method for lawyers to use in ethically responding to hostile communications, correcting misinformation from others, and initiating productive correspondence. The BIFF Response method can also be used by other law office personnel such as paralegals and legal secretaries. with dozens of examples of responses to common situations involving hostile or misinformed emails, text messages, and other forms of communication. BIFF stands for *brief, informative, friendly, and firm.*

The BIFF Response method can also be taught to clients to help them write their own friendly and concise responses in their cases, which saves lawyers time and reduces the escalation of unnecessary conflicts during their case. This book explains how to coach office staff, clients, and their family members to use the BIFF method, including ten key questions to ask when reviewing their correspondence. While this method is designed primarily for written communication, it can also be used in verbal conversations, to be efficient and respectful.

The book is divided into five parts: (1) learning the BIFF method, (2) correspondence with clients, (3) correspondence with colleagues, (4) correspondence with staff and between staff, and (5) coaching staff and clients. Each scenario begins with a hostile or misinformed correspondence received by the lawyer and/or staff member, then gives a tempting response which is not quite a BIFF (analyzed using the BIFF Checker), then gives a sample communication that *is* a BIFF.

We already know that we *should be* civil in our communications in the practice of law. This is a book about *how* to be civil while protecting our clients and ourselves at the same time.

Who We Are

Before we get into the nuts and bolts of BIFF communications, we'd like to introduce ourselves and the origins of (and need for) this method.

Bill

Soon after I became a lawyer in 1992, an associate justice of the California Supreme Court gave a talk to a gathering of lawyers at our local bar association in San Diego. The justice included his concerns about the diminishing civility in the legal profession. This surprised me because I thought I was entering a collegial profession, after previously being in the relatively friendly profession of therapists for twelve years. The lawyers I had met so far were welcoming and seemed to get along well. While lawyer jokes were becoming popular, I was unaware that lawyers were treating each other badly within the profession. Well, it didn't take long before I started getting my share of highly offensive letters and emails from opposing counsel, although it was a small fraction of lawyers who seemed to communicate like this on a regular basis.

It didn't get better; it got worse. Over the years, I collected a stack of my favorite nasty-grams from certain opposing counsel, as well as from some clients, their family members, and people I didn't even know who needed someone to blame. An early one I remember was a four-page diatribe from opposing counsel in response to my request that he respond to a settlement proposal. It included sentences like "I have bigger fish to fry than to respond to you, and I will get to it when I'm ready." He could easily have sent me a four-page response to our settlement proposal in the time it took to harangue me. Of course, he never sent a settlement response, and we had to go to trial. Over time, all caps and exclamation marks started coming into style, as well as personal insults about morals, intelligence, ethics, and wondering how you were let into the profession. You may already know what I'm talking about, and if you haven't seen this yet, you may soon.

In 2006, the new president of the California State Bar Association expressed his concerns about the lack of civility. So, in 2007, the State Bar issued its *California Attorney Guidelines of Civility and Professionalism,* which was separate from and in addition to the rules of professional conduct. These seemed great, but there was one problem: they weren't mandatory. They had no teeth to enforce them. Instead, they counted on goodwill. Here's what their FAQs sheet said about that:

> *8. If they are not mandatory, why should an attorney abide by the Guidelines?* Civility in the practice of law promotes effectiveness and enjoyment of the practice of law. They also promote economical client representation. Conversely, uncivil conduct not only disserves clients, it demeans the profession and the American system of justice.[1]

By then I had already written and published my book *High-Conflict People in Legal Disputes* (2006). In it I described some of the patterns of high-conflict personalities, one of which is that they rarely change, and another is that many lack empathy and remorse. So, high-conflict lawyers were already demonstrating that they cared more about themselves than about the profession and system of justice. Without strong consequences, those lawyers who were uncivil would just continue, and the rest of lawyers who were already civil (90 percent, in my opinion) didn't need printed rules to know how to behave. Thus, the guidelines seemed to miss the target. I wrote an article about this problem for the statewide *California Family Law News,*

---

1 State Bar of California, *California Attorney Guidelines of Civility and Professionalism,* Adopted by the Board of Governors on July 20, 2007, FAQs, 2.

"Misunderstanding Incivility and How to Stop It," which is appendix A to this book.

Needless to say, these efforts at defining civility had zero impact on the problem, as I predicted. Reasonable lawyers and their staff struggled with how to respond to these uncivil communications and often tried to admonish their colleagues in a way that ended up being seen as insulting and mutually inappropriate. Was it better to write back nastily or not respond at all? This was important to figure out, since so much of our work is done in writing and most cases settle out of court based significantly on written communications.

Because of my background as a therapist before I became a lawyer, I often counseled my law clients on how to communicate in writing with their angry spouses, family members, bosses, and others in order to manage the situation and keep things as calm as possible. I didn't really think about what I was telling them, but I knew whether their emails needed to be changed or not as soon as I saw them. Many of my colleagues were also rewriting their clients' emails, especially in family law matters.

It all came together for me in March 2007. I was giving a two-day training on managing high-conflict personalities with my colleague Megan Hunter, who had worked for the Arizona Supreme Court as their family law specialist with judicial trainings and other projects as an administrator (not a lawyer). There were family lawyers, therapists, mediators, and two judges in attendance at that training. One of the judges asked me how we could stop these awful emails that the parties were writing to each other and filing in court. I suggested that the communication should be brief, informative (without emotional commentary), and friendly. One judge said, "That spells BIF. If you add another F, you have BIFF." So, I suggested that the emails also needed to be firm, meaning that they ended the hostile conversation. Thus, BIFF was born—and soon trademarked as the BIFF Response.

In 2008, Megan and I cofounded High Conflict Institute and dedicated ourselves full-time to training professionals in understanding and managing their high-conflict clients and cases. BIFF became one of several key methods that we and our other trainers now teach around the world. We developed a ten-question checklist for coaching people in how to use it and published three BIFF books: *BIFF: Quick Responses to High-Conflict People* (2011, 2014); *BIFF for CoParent Communication* (2020); and *BIFF at Work* (2021).

The response has been stunning. People love BIFFing the difficult people in their lives and showing us their BIFFs. And when both parties to a conflict communicate in this way, they tend to both calm down even more. How simple! We estimate that our trainers and books have taught over half a million people how to use the BIFF Response method in their written (and sometimes verbal) communication. One surprising outcome is that most people who have learned this method have taught it to at least one other person, which means over one million people worldwide are likely to be using BIFF now.

In 2021, Megan and I met Rehana Jamal, a graduate student at the Straus Institute for Dispute Resolution at Pepperdine University's School of Law (where I teach a course in Psychology of Conflict Communication once a year). Rehana contacted us about doing an externship with our High Conflict Institute. She was such a perfect fit that we hired her to work with us after her externship program ended, and she graduated with her master's in the Dispute Resolution program. She was already a lawyer with a couple years' experience, so she helped us develop our certification program in High Conflict Legal Dispute Resolution, which is now available on demand with Live Lab practice sessions.

Rehana's next project was coauthoring this book. She brings the perspective of a young and relatively new lawyer to this project, which we hope is reassuring to those just getting started in this often-challenging profession. She has helped expand this book to cover many situations in a wide range of settings that any lawyer, staff, or other professional can relate to. (See appendix B for a list of examples in different settings and situations.) I have enjoyed collaborating with her on this project. Now it's her turn.

Rehana

I am writing as a conflict-resolution specialist and attorney. Prior to entering the world of conflict resolution, I was a practicing immigration attorney. I worked at a nonprofit in New York City and constantly dealt with other attorneys, court staff, experts, and other professionals associated with my clients' cases. The biggest problem that I came across was issues relating to communication: miscommunication, lack of communication, and strained channels of communication. As a young attorney, I sometimes felt inadequately equipped to deal with these issues. What was more shocking to me was that I witnessed other experienced attorneys who also were not adequately skilled in communication, and this led to major conflicts that could have been avoided.

As I transitioned to a career in conflict resolution, my time at the Straus Institute for Dispute Resolution helped me see how employing simple conflict-resolution skills in the work environment could shift people's attitudes and mindsets. I also saw how changes in tone, length of communication, and language could enhance interactions. Many of the issues that I encountered as a young attorney could have been easily resolved with the skills I learned during my time at Pepperdine University, including BIFF.

It was in one of my courses that I learned of BIFF. I brushed it off at first, thinking it was another quick fix, but for some reason, "brief, informative, friendly, and firm" stuck with me. I started thinking of BIFF even when I was writing personal emails and saw how the manner in which I shifted my communication style had a direct effect on the type of responses I received. I also started thinking back on past communications I'd had as an attorney, especially communicating with opposing counsel, and wishing that I'd had BIFF in those days. Now I can't imagine a world without BIFF, and I am excited to share it with others in the legal field.

Our Hopes

Together, we hope to give you tools and confidence in dealing with the angry and misinformed communications that will certainly come your way. We also hope to give your colleagues and staff a method of calming conflict that is accessible to everyone. When everyone around you uses the BIFF Response method, life sure is easier in this modern world of conflict and law.

We wish you all the best in your BIFF responses!

Bill Eddy, LCSW, Esq.
Rehana Jamal, Esq.
January 2024

PART 1

Learning the BIFF Method

CHAPTER 1

Blamespeak and High-Conflict Personalities

Have you ever received an email, text, or letter that said something like this:

> *"You are irresponsible and unethical! How can you sleep at night?"*

> *"How long have you been practicing law? You don't seem to know the first thing!"*

> *"Do you know what your client did this weekend!!! You need to fix it NOW!!!"*

> *"I told you. I'M NOT GOING TO AGREE TO ANYTHING THAT MY EX PROPOSES!"*

> *"If that's how you're going to be, I'LL SEE YOU IN COURT! TOMORROW!"*

> *"You tell your boss that you should be fired! You're totally incompetent!"*

> *"It's ALL your fault!"*

Blamespeak is the term we coined in 2010 to describe the language of our new culture of blame that was growing rapidly around the world. And it's just getting worse, not better. It is rampant on the internet, in entertainment, in the news, in politics, in families, at work, and especially in the practice of law. To understand the problem that the BIFF Response addresses, it helps to first understand blamespeak and why people—especially those with high-conflict personalities—engage in it. This will help you know what *not* to write from the start.

Blamespeak is not about you! It's about the writer (or speaker) and their lack of problem-solving skills, not an indication that you have done anything wrong. Even if you have made a mistake or omission or didn't understand something, blamespeak is totally out of proportion and not geared to finding solutions. So, don't take it personally, and try not to get emotionally hooked or reactive. BIFF will help you with this.

How Blamespeak Hooks Us

Blamespeak can easily hook your brain, shutting down any rational responses and triggering defensiveness and a "fight, flight, or freeze" response. See if any of this sounds familiar to you:

1. It's usually **emotionally intense** and out of proportion to the issues. Sometimes it can seem calm but be subtle and passive-aggressive and bring out the worst in a reasonable person's response. It grabs your defensive brain because it feels like an attack. That's because it *is* an attack. It's emotional, as compared to logical problem solving. You *feel* in danger.

2. It's **very personal**: about your intelligence, sanity, memory, ethics, sex life, looks, race, age, and so forth.

3. It's **"all your fault:"** the blamespeaker feels no responsibility for the problem or the solution and sees things in all-or-nothing terms.

4. It's **out of context**: it ignores all of the good you've done and all of the bad the blamespeaker has done.

5. It's often **shared with others** (they are often copied in on the communication) to emphasize how blameworthy you

are and how blameless the speaker is. The blamespeaker may have no sense of shame, embarrassment, or boundaries. He or she may speak this way about you in public. Unfortunately, blamespeak often sounds believable to those who aren't informed about your situation. If you believe that others agree with the blamespeaker, you will feel even more defensive. You will feel outnumbered.

6. You have an **intensely negative gut feeling** about the blamespeak, which sickens you, makes you feel intensely fearful, suddenly helpless, and/or very angry at someone: the blamespeaker or another one of their targets of blame.

7. You find yourself **compelled to respond with blamespeak** of your own. It is extremely hard to step back to prepare a reasonable response, or to decide not to respond at all.[2]

The important thing is to recognize this pattern of behavior and avoid reacting to it. New lawyers and employees are particularly susceptible to absorbing blamespeak and feeling like they have to react right away. Remember, it's not about you and your skills and abilities; it's about the blamespeaker's lack of problem-solving skills. BIFF communications will help you pause and choose an effective response.

High-Conflict Personalities

Some people slip into blamespeak accidently and momentarily. They may even apologize for it. You may have even used blamespeak on occasion and regretted it afterward. Or you may have thought it was the only way to respond even though you don't usually communicate that way.

But some people chronically use blamespeak as their way of relating to others. It's an enduring pattern of behavior that

---

2 This list of seven characteristics of blamespeak first appeared in *BIFF: Quick Responses to High Conflict People, Their Personal Attacks, Hostile Email and Social Media Meltdowns* (Scottsdale, AZ: Unhooked Books, 2011), 12–13.

may be part of their personality—the way they think, feel, and act in the world. We think of people who regularly increase the intensity of conflicts or prolong conflicts this way as having *high-conflict personalities* or being high-conflict people (HCPs). They tend to have four primary characteristics:

Preoccupation with blaming others
(without taking responsibility themselves)

Lots of all-or-nothing thinking
(and all-or-nothing solutions to problems)

Unmanaged or intense emotions
(which can completely take over)

Extreme behavior or threats
(things 90 percent of people would never do).

They also may have a *personality disorder* or traits of such a disorder. People with personality disorders have "an enduring pattern of inner experience and behavior that deviates markedly from the expectations of the individual's culture." They often have difficulties with how they think (misperceiving themselves, others, and events), how they manage their emotions (difficulty keeping them in proportion to events), interpersonal functioning, and impulse control.[3] These disorders are beyond the scope of this book, but understanding the high-conflict behavior they entail is enough to help you know how to focus your communication.

Note: Don't ever tell someone you think they are a high-conflict person or have a personality disorder, or they will make your life miserable for weeks or months or years. Besides, you might not be right. Instead, it's better to stay calm and use the methods in this book and other books about HCPs. Resources can be found at www.highconflictinstitute.com.

---

3   American Psychiatric Association (APA): *Diagnostic and Statistical Manual of Mental Disorders, Fifth Edition, Text Revision.* Washington, DC, American Psychiatric Association, 2022, 734.

It's important to note that not all people with personality disorders are high-conflict people. Many do not focus on a *target of blame*. And not all people with high-conflict personalities have personality disorders, which means they may not be as firmly stuck in a pattern of dysfunctional behavior and may be slightly more able to achieve insight and change. Here's a comparison of these personalities:

PERSONALITY DISORDERS	HIGH-CONFLICT PEOPLE
Enduring pattern of interpersonal dysfunction	Preoccupied with Target(s) of Blame
Lacks self-reflection	All-or-nothing thinking
Externalizes responsibility	Unmanaged emotions
Rarely or never changes behavior	Extreme behavior or threats

One particular cluster of personality disorders in the mental health diagnostic manual (DSM-5-TR) that frequently become involved in legal disputes is Cluster B: narcissistic, antisocial, borderline, and histrionic. These are described in the DSM-5-TR as often appearing "dramatic, emotional, or erratic." In addition, research shows that personality disorders are primarily *interpersonal disorders,* such that many more people than the individual with the disorder are affected by them— and often quite negatively. In an article in *Psychological Bulletin,* authors Sylia Wilson, Catherine B. Stroud, and C. Emily Durbin write:

"A growing body of empirical research has also considered associations between personality disorders and the quality of functioning in specific interpersonal relationships, such as with one's **children, parents and siblings, peers, and romantic partners.**"[4]

"Antisocial, borderline, histrionic, and narcissistic personality disorders, historically classified as Cluster B (dramatic-emotional-erratic) personality disorders, all showed moderate-to-large and significant associations with **domineeringness, vindictiveness, and intrusiveness.**"[5]

"Interestingly, each of the personality disorders showed a significant association with vindictiveness, speaking to a commonality across the personality disorders in a tendency toward distrust and suspicion of others and an **inability to care about the needs of others.**"[6] (Emphasis added)

This seems to describe many of the people in today's legal cases, including our clients, family members, and other professionals—sometimes even opposing counsel. It doesn't matter what position a person is in; if they have a personality disorder, that will dictate their behavior more than their profession or other role in society will.

Negative Advocates

One thing to be aware of with high-conflict people is that they tend to consciously or unconsciously recruit *negative advocates*: people who will fight for them without necessarily knowing the

4 Sylia Wilson, Catherine B. Stroud, and C. Emily Durbin, "Interpersonal Dysfunction in Personality Disorders: A Meta-Analytic Review," *Psychological Bulletin*, July 2017; 143(7): 677-734, 2/71. doi: 10.1037/bul0000101. https://pubmed.ncbi.nlm.nih.gov/28447827/

5 *Id.* at 20/71.

6 *Id.* at 35/71.

facts of the case. Negative advocates can make your job much harder. They are most often family members, but they can also be friends, coworkers, and even professionals. They get emotionally hooked into advocating for the high-conflict person's thinking, emotions, and behavior.

Negative advocates can try to take over the case if you're not careful about setting boundaries. Yet they often don't understand the true details of the case and operate emotionally in an all-or-nothing manner on behalf of their high-conflict person. In other words, they act like a high-conflict person even though they may ordinarily be a reasonable person. Lawyers and therapists are particularly prone to becoming negative advocates, so be careful about this in your cases. Also be aware that you may have to deal with these negative-advocate professionals in the same way you communicate with a high-conflict person.

The Four Fuhgeddaboudits

Once you recognize high-conflict characteristics in another person, don't try to change them! Adapt how *you* interact with them to accommodate their inability to solve problems and conflicts in a normal way. There are four specific things to avoid. We call them the Four Fuhgeddaboudits:

Forget about trying to give them insight into themselves. We recommend this because they are highly defensive and interpret any feedback about their behavior—no matter how well-intentioned—to be a hostile attack. They typically think with the right brain, which leads to defensiveness, meaning that insight (primarily a left-brain activity) just won't occur.

Forget about focusing on the past. Focus instead on what to do now and in the future. They have been getting negative feedback about their behavior all their lives, and they aren't going to change now. You may need to talk about some past problem, but focus most of your attention and information on current and future solutions.

Forget about opening up emotions. High-conflict people tend to carry a lot of powerful unresolved emotions around with them. Also, their ways of interacting with people generally don't work, so they are constantly feeling frustrated, helpless, vulnerable, weak, and like a victim. If you ask how they are feeling, they will usually tell you that they feel awful—and then possibly focus their frustration or anger on you. It's better to stay focused on thinking and doing: thinking of solutions and doing what needs to be done next.

Forget about labeling them. Avoid calling them a "high-conflict person" or "someone with a personality disorder" or any other unnecessary name. Many people have done that in an effort to motivate them or shame them into better behavior, but it never works, and it worsens your relationship with them. Stay focused on choices and thinking and doing.

Conclusion

People with high-conflict personalities—and their negative advocates—typically engage in aggressive, emotionally charged communication. It's tempting to fight back against what often feels like a personal attack, but if the person has a high-conflict personality, doing so will make things worse, not better, for you. While it's not always easy to do, there is great benefit in *not responding in kind* to hostile communications. You can often decide whether the conflict will escalate, diminish, or end by how you respond to the other person's blamespeak. It's up to you!

CHAPTER 2

The BIFF Method: Brief, Informative, Friendly, and Firm

The BIFF communication method is your answer to blame-speak. It's designed to be applied in writing, but it can be used verbally as well. We focus in this book on written communication such as emails, texts, letters, and memos. While originally created for *responding* to a hostile communication (hence the name "BIFF Response"), the BIFF method can also be used to *initiate* a written conversation based on the same four characteristics. To be a BIFF, a communication must be:

Brief. Typically, we recommend that you write just a paragraph, or four to six sentences. This makes it less likely that you will include something that will trigger the other person's blamespeak. This guideline applies even if you are responding to a several-page letter or multi-paragraph email. Remember, this isn't a trial brief that needs to cover every issue raised point by point. Brevity also reduces the amount of time you may be tempted to spend on responding.

Informative. Just provide the necessary information, without any arguments, emotions, opinions, or defenses. (You don't need to defend yourself, and doing so usually aggravates a high-conflict person and escalates the situation). Usually, you can simply provide accurate information on the subject without having to tear down their point of view or argument. Focusing on logistics—such as Who, What, Where, and When—can often help.

Friendly. You don't have to be super friendly, but it helps to set a cordial tone at the start. You can do this with a sentence such as "Thank you for letting me know your concerns" or "Thank you for responding to my request." Sometimes it helps to add a sentence showing empathy or respect for the person, such as "I know this is a hard time, and I appreciate your flexibility" or "I respect your time, so I'm keeping this brief." You may sometimes wish to put a nice comment at the end, like "Have a good weekend."

Firm. Ultimately, the purpose of a BIFF is to try to end the hostile conversation. Don't put any hooks out, like "What do you think of that, buddy!" Being firm doesn't mean being harsh. The best BIFFs don't even get a response, because they're so effective in ending the hostile exchange. On the other hand, sometimes you will need to ask for a response. If you do, try to end your BIFF communication with a simple question, such as a yes-or-no query with a requested response date and time, so you're not waiting forever.

The BIFF method gives you a way to respond productively to provocative communications from high-conflict people. It can help bring hostile conversations to an end while minimizing frustration and wasted time.

The Three A's

In addition to the four characteristics of a BIFF, we have three additional pitfalls to avoid. We call them the Three A's:

Advice. It's not effective to include unsolicited advice in a response to an angry person. This isn't usually what they are asking for, and it can quickly escalate a conflict that you're trying to calm down. Lawyers especially have a hard time resisting the urge to do this, as we regularly give advice as part of our jobs. But unwanted, unsolicited advice triggers clients, opposing counsel, and others. "Let me give you some advice here…" is very easy to say, but it's often a big mistake. In general, and with high-conflict people especially, it's best to ask if they want some advice before giving it. When they're angry with you is not the time to do it. Remember that you are trying to keep this brief.

Admonishment. This goes beyond advice in talking down to a person. This is also very tempting for lawyers, and also a big mistake. No one likes to be talked down to. Save this for judges to do in court and parents to do with their five-year-olds. Admonishing opposing counsel on how to communicate will usually not improve their communication. Skip it.

Apologies. This is perhaps the most surprising tip we can give you. In many situations, an apology can go a long way to solving a problem or resolving a dispute. However, when you're dealing with a high-conflict person or simply someone who is angry with you, giving them an apology in writing may just be giving them ammunition to use against you in the future. Keep in mind that they often tend toward all-or-nothing thinking, so that if you apologize for something small, they may hear that you agree that it's "all your fault!"

For example, suppose that you had a hearing that went poorly and you're writing your client afterward. You might be tempted to write "Well, that approach didn't work. Sorry about that!" This could form the basis of a demand for a reduction in fees, firing you as their lawyer, or even suing you for malpractice. If you have a potentially high-conflict client, you want to avoid saying things like that, because such clients are not objective about analyzing what went wrong and learning how to handle their case more effectively. Instead, they are preoccupied with seeing the world through all-or-nothing glasses, so whatever happened is now the worst thing in the world. So, focus on what to do next. Remember the second Fuhgeddaboudit from the previous chapter: Avoid focusing on the past. Focus on the future.

Sometimes you may be tempted to say you are sorry to see your clients in the situation they are in. You can always say that you are saddened, which is often true. "I'm saddened to see that you're in this horrible situation. Let's see what we can do about it." This is better than saying you're sorry, which may be interpreted as acknowledging that it is somehow your fault.

Of course, there are times when an apology is truly appropriate or necessary. For example, if you or your organization have made a mistake that is affecting a large number of people or the public, an apology may be essential to resolving or calming the situation, and most people aren't high-conflict people. They will appreciate an apology and see it for what it is. Think this through carefully, and make sure to get at least one other person's opinion on how an apology statement reads.

In a routine BIFF communication, steer clear of apologies for the reasons above.

Once you've composed an email, text, or letter that is brief, informative, friendly, and firm, ask yourself if you've done any of the Three A's. Have you given advice? Are your words an admonishment? Have you apologized? These are important questions to ask yourself or someone you are coaching in the BIFF method.

Do You Need to Respond?

Now that you know what a BIFF communication looks like, how do you know if you need to use one at all? This question is often where you should start. The answer depends on the situation.

With clients, you should usually respond to their concerns for good lawyer-client relations. Using a BIFF Response will help you keep it brief. A nice BIFF is usually better than no response at all.

With opposing counsel and other professionals, it is also wise to respond in order to keep a good relationship with them. A simple BIFF communication can help strengthen your rapport, especially if it is addressing a difficult subject in a respectful manner.

With self-representing opposing parties, you should always communicate in the BIFF format. This is a skillful alternative to getting nasty or ignoring them.

With family members and friends of a client, who you respond to can make a difference. You should check with your client about whether or not to respond to family and friends. They may be helpful in calming and managing your client, or they may be disruptive or on bad terms. It may be better to not respond and have your client deal with them, so they don't become a disruptive influence in the case and waste your time. It usually depends on whether they are a positive or negative person in the case.

If the other party responds to your BIFF, do you need to keep responding? With clients, colleagues, and others, we recommend that you reply once more but more briefly and say you won't be responding further on this topic. Then if they write back again, you are in a better position to not respond.

Of course, you'll need to be flexible about applying all of these suggestions. Decide for yourself if they fit a specific situation.

More Than One Way

BIFF communications allow for a lot of flexibility. Two people may write completely different responses to the same hostile or misinformed communication, and both will be BIFFs, as long as they are brief, informative, friendly, and firm. Different people will naturally emphasize different things. In addition, many communications have more than one piece of content, each of which could be addressed in more than one way. For example, someone might have raised an unrelated issue in their email or text message. You will need to decide whether to address that issue, simply acknowledge it, or ignore it. This question is best answered by considering these three things:

1) Who the reader is.
2) Who the writer is.
3) What the situation is.

You probably know the reader, so you can picture how he or she will respond to what you have written after you have drafted it. You may realize that what you wrote needs to be toned down a bit, or that there's something that needs more explanation. As for the writer, hopefully you know yourself well enough to communicate in such a way that you don't accidentally push the other person's button unnecessarily. Understanding the situation may help you decide whether the current issue needs more or less discussion and whether your communication is likely to end up in court, which can influence what you write and whether to ignore an issue or not. Generally, less is more.

Pause or Get Feedback Before You Send (If You Can)

If you have received a particularly upsetting email or text message, it can help to pause for an hour or a day before you send your response. Our brains take a little time to calm down and get the cortisol and adrenaline out of our systems. You also are less likely to speed up the other person's next response, thereby giving their brain a rest as well.

If you can, have someone else look at your response before you send it. In legal disputes, a hasty email can have a long-term negative effect. We all know of cases in which emails exposed a company or individual to liability because of their nastiness or disclosure of confidential information. People have been fired for their impulsive inappropriate communications. With electronic discovery rules, you can't just take it back or delete it without severe consequences. Everything must be preserved. It's better to pause and think ahead. If someone else does look over your draft, encourage them to coach you on it using the ten questions that we cover in chapter 19.

Of course, you can ask yourself if what you have written is really brief, informative, friendly, and firm. By the time you finish this book, you will have a clear idea of what a good BIFF communication can look like. It gets easier and easier with practice.

Conclusion

BIFF communications are simple but can be harder than they look at first. With practice, you can use this format in more and more effective ways for any written communication. You will often know how successful you were by the response you get, or by the lack of a response, which is often the sign of an effective BIFF Response. Remember that the goal is to shut down a hostile or unnecessary written conversation. In general, less is more when responding to an aggressive or misinformed person. By doing your best to be brief, informative, friendly, and firm, you can calm conflicts or prevent them altogether. By avoiding the Three A's, you can further keep things from escalating into excessive conflict or making yourself unnecessarily vulnerable to someone who may try to use your words against you.

Now let's look at how you can quickly check your communication to see if it's a BIFF.

CHAPTER 3

The Quick-and-Simple BIFF Checker

After you have written a draft response or first message in a conversation, it helps to use the BIFF Checker before you hit Send. The BIFF Checker includes the four characteristics of a BIFF plus the Three A's. The following example demonstrates how to use the BIFF Checker. This will be the format of the examples in the chapters throughout this book. First, we help you catch problems with what has been written, showing why something is not a BIFF communication. Then, we offer one way to rewrite the draft as a BIFF communication, with a brief explanation of why. Keep in mind that there is no one right way to write a BIFF. Several different ways may work, so long as they are brief, informative, friendly, and firm.

Document Not Sent

Let's look at an example of how you can check a written communication before you send it. We'll start with a common lawyer-client situation, then put it through the BIFF Checker.

From: Reena Patel (client)
To: Richard Thomas (attorney)
CC: Sarah Singh (legal assistant)
Subject: Settlement Proposal

Hey Mr. Thomas!

It's been two weeks, and I am still waiting on a copy of my settlement proposal. WHERE IS IT??? Your assistant said she would send it to me a week ago. After we spent weeks working on this proposal, I cannot believe you don't have the courtesy to follow up! We have had endless phone calls and meetings about this proposal, and I do not understand why it is not finalized. THIS IS COMPLETELY IRRESPONSIBLE.

I am kindly asking you to send it to me by tonight. I thought we had a good working relationship, and now I am wondering if I can work with you again. This is unacceptable. I really don't know how we proceed from here!!

Reena

Response 1

From: Richard Thomas
To: Reena Patel
CC: Sarah Singh
Subject: RE: Settlement Proposal

Dear Ms. Patel,
I'm sure we sent the settlement agreement last week. I would advise you to recheck your email. Our office is very timely, and we are not in the practice of withholding documents.

Kindly check again.

Best,

Richard Thomas

BIFF CHECKER: YES OR NO

IS A RESPONSE NECESSARY?	Yes	It's always important to respond to client emails (if you want to get paid and keep the client).
BRIEF? (2 to 5 sentences)	Yes	It is a brief response.
INFORMATIVE? (who, what, when, where, what for)	No	It's purely defensive and blaming, without providing any information about the problem.
FRIENDLY?	No	The attorney used words like "kindly" and "best," but the overall tone is passive-aggressive and not friendly.
FIRM?	No	The response is firm in that it is intended to end the angry conversation. But is likely to trigger a new negative response and escalate the conflict.
ADVICE?	Yes	The lawyer condescendingly advises the client.
ADMONISHMENTS?	Yes	There are passive-aggressive admonishments in which the lawyer places blame on the client.
APOLOGIES?	No	The attorney does not apologize, but he starts to blame the client and takes no responsibility or corrective measures in this case, and this won't be effective either.

IS IT A BIFF? NO

Response 2

From: Richard Thomas
To: Reena Patel
CC: Sarah Singh
Subject: RE: Settlement Proposal

Dear Ms. Patel,

Thank you for drawing my attention to this matter. I discovered that there was an oversight in sending you the settlement proposal. (Ms. Singh was out of the office on Friday and I didn't realize it didn't go out. I'll make sure this doesn't happen again.) I am attaching a copy of the proposal here.

I am happy to discuss any additions or modifications you would like.

Best wishes,

Richard Thomas

BIFF CHECKER: YES OR NO

IS A RESPONSE NECESSARY?	Yes	She is a client.
BRIEF? (2 to 5 sentences)	Yes	It is brief and to the point.
INFORMATIVE? (who, what, when, where, what for)	Yes	It explains what happened, provides information about the next steps, and leaves space for questions and modifications.
FRIENDLY?	Yes	The first sentence acknowledges that there was an oversight by the attorney and reassures the client that there are measures in place to allow for better follow-up in the future. He is open to additions or modifications.

FIRM?	Yes	It is designed to end the hostile conversation and resolve the issue.
ADVICE?	No	
ADMONISHMENTS?	No	
APOLOGIES?	No	Rather than apologizing, the attorney acknowledges and briefly explains what occurred. He takes responsibility for ensuring better follow-up in the future, but very briefly so that he doesn't open the door to an argument about it.

IS IT A BIFF? YES

This example shows that checking your writing can be done very quickly. By using the BIFF Checker, you can catch possible inflammatory or unnecessary words that you might otherwise miss. Many people have this list of eight questions posted by their computer to remind them to check before they hit Send.

Write It Your Way

As we mentioned above, you might address this issue with slightly different words, and it could still be a BIFF communication. You can try it now: Take any response or anything you have written to start a conversation and run it through this BIFF Checker. Feel free to copy the following two pages for your own use.

BIFF CHECKER: YES OR NO

IS A RESPONSE NECESSARY?		With clients, opposing counsel, or others involved in a case, it is usually best to respond. But occasionally, no response is necessary.
BRIEF? (2 to 5 sentences)		A communication should usually be just one paragraph, even if you are responding to a lengthy email or letter. Remember, this method is designed for correspondence, not a trial brief in which you may need to respond to every single item.
INFORMATIVE? (who, what, when, where, what for)		It should be focused on logistical or fact-focused information, such as who did or will do what, where, and when. Avoid defenses, emotions, judgments, arguments, and criticisms. Avoid pointing out where the other person is wrong; just explain what is true.
FRIENDLY?		There can be a friendly greeting ("Thanks for letting me know your concerns") or closing ("Have a nice weekend"). It does not have to be overly friendly, since you want to be brief and maintain professionalism. Also, some high-conflict people will try to manipulate you if you try too hard to be friendly.
FIRM?		The communication is meant to resolve the issue and end the hostile conversation. It can include a yes-or-no question, with an expected response date and time, and still be a BIFF.

ADVICE?	Avoid if the other person is not asking for advice. Remember that unsolicited advice is very likely to trigger defensiveness and a new, angry response.
ADMONISHMENTS?	Avoid admonishments. They are especially likely to trigger more hostility. No one likes to be talked down to like a child. Admonishing someone may feel good for about twenty seconds, but it will cause more problems in the long run.
APOLOGIES?	Avoid apologizing to possible high-conflict people. Remember, they may assume this means you agree that it's "all your fault," and they may use your apology as ammunition against you. It's okay to briefly explain how a problem occurred and assure them that it will be handled better in the future.

IS IT A BIFF?

Rewrite What You Have Received

Sometimes people find it helpful to rewrite the initial correspondence that they received, before responding to it.

You can rewrite it as a BIFF, to see if there is anything useful in it to respond to. For example, if you took this approach to the client email above, it might look like this:

Hey Mr. Thomas!

~~It's been two weeks, and~~ I am still waiting on a copy of my settlement proposal. ~~WHERE IS IT??? Your assistant said she would send it to me a week ago. After we spent weeks working on this proposal, I cannot believe you don't have the courtesy to follow up! We have had endless phone calls and meetings about this proposal, and I do not understand why it is not finalized. THIS IS COMPLETELY IRRESPONSIBLE.~~

I am kindly asking you to send it to me by tonight. ~~I thought we had a good working relationship, and now I am wondering if I can work with you again. This is unacceptable. I really don't know how we proceed from here!!~~

Reena

This often distills a communication into a much less emotional message, which triggers much less of an emotional response within you. It can be fun to do this, since it points out how absurd and unproductive many of the sentences are in an angry email. It's also good practice on how to write a BIFF.

Conclusion

The remaining chapters will apply this quick-and-simple approach in evaluating your initial written communications or your responses to hostile or misinformed communications. Keep in mind that it is often helpful to have another person review your communication before you send it. (See chapter 19 on how to coach each other.) If what you have received is particularly inflammatory or outrageously misinformed, it can also help to pause a few minutes, an hour, or a day before sending so that you can calm down and consider your response. Now, let's look at many different types of common communication situations in which you can apply the BIFF method.

PART 2

Correspondence with Clients

CHAPTER 4

Responding to Upset Clients

A lot of the communications initiated by clients are driven by stress, fear, and misunderstandings. Clients—especially high-conflict clients—may lash out at their lawyers or law office staff on a regular basis about minor issues as well as major ones.

Should You Respond?

You should almost always reply to client emails, letters, and other communications. However, it helps to explain from the start of your working relationship how you can best communicate with each other. Let the client know how routine information and urgent matters should be provided to you: by email, voicemail, or a message to a member of your support staff. Taking a few extra minutes at the beginning to explain how you work will save a lot of your own time and stress throughout the case.

Early in your working relationship, it is often advisable to take the client's first "crisis" phone call, so you can reassure the client that you are there for them. However, you can also make clear that you cannot always reply right away, so putting messages in writing may be helpful for both of you. You can also let them know that setting up a conference call or meeting may be more appropriate. An occasional reassuring email or phone call throughout the case can help clients understand which issues are important and which can be ignored. By using a BIFF Response, you can keep it brief, save time, and avoid increasing your own stress—while significantly calming a client.

Let's take a look at some examples.

Stressed Client

From: Samantha Meyer (client)
To: Ari Goldman (attorney)
Subject: Please respond!

Hello Mr. Goldman,

I have called you three times this week, and this is my second email WITHOUT A RESPONSE! My ex-husband has tried to contact me, even though we are in divorce proceedings and I told him to only communicate through our lawyers. I am extremely upset, and I need to move this process along faster. You told me that I could call or email you when something urgent comes up. THIS IS URGENT.

This is a really uncomfortable situation for me because prior to our divorce, we were already on bad terms. Things have only gotten worse with time. This has been a really difficult time for me, and I was counting on your support in this process. I really can't have contact with my ex during this process, and I really need you to end this soon.

Please return my calls and emails!

Thanks,

Samantha

Response 1

From: Ari Goldman (attorney)
To: Samantha Meyer (client)
Subject: RE: Please respond!

Hello Samantha,

We have talked about this before. You need to be discerning

---

when deciding what is and what is not an emergency. We had a similar type of call last week. I am doing everything that I can to move this divorce process along. I will call you when there are any updates. I obviously do not want to cut off communication with you, but I have other clients as well.

Wait for me to contact you next week with updates.

Thanks,

Ari, Esq.

BIFF CHECKER: YES OR NO

IS A RESPONSE NECESSARY?	Yes	It is almost always necessary to respond to a client.
BRIEF? (2 to 5 sentences)	Yes	The email is fairly brief.
INFORMATIVE? (who, what, when, where, what for)	Yes	The email does explain the situation. Note that the attorney includes unnecessary details as well, which may be counterproductive.
FRIENDLY?	No	It is clear that the attorney is frustrated and tired of having the same conversation. While he has used some friendly language ("Hello" and "Thanks"), the overall tone of the email is tense.
FIRM?	Yes	The email is firm. It clearly states what should happen next, so there is no need for the client to respond.
ADVICE?	Yes	The attorney advises the client about what to do next, since they have clearly had this conversation before.

| ADMONISHMENTS? | Yes | The attorney admonishes the client for her frequent communication. This is a fair admonishment, but the way the attorney says it has a negative impact. |
| APOLOGIES? | No | No apologies. |

IS IT A BIFF? NO

Response 2

From: Ari Goldman (attorney)
To: Samantha Meyer (client)
Subject: RE: Please respond!

Hello Samantha,

I understand that you are frustrated by this situation. I can assure you that I am doing what I can to move along the divorce process. I do my best to return client calls, and as we agreed, we will continue to have our weekly check-ins.

I will call you on Monday, and we can discuss ongoing issues in the case.

Thank you,

Ari

BIFF CHECKER: YES OR NO

IS A RESPONSE NECESSARY?	Yes	It is almost always necessary to respond to a client.
BRIEF? (2 to 5 sentences)	Yes	The attorney gives only the necessary information and a reminder of agreed-upon terms.
INFORMATIVE? (who, what, when, where, what for)	Yes	The attorney addresses everything the client raised and reminds her that they have an agreement in place to have weekly check-ins.
FRIENDLY?	Yes	The email is friendly and neutral. The attorney acknowledges the client's frustration.
FIRM?	Yes	The attorney makes it clear that their agreed-upon weekly check-ins are the proper space to discuss ongoing issues. This sets a limit and does not leave room for further back-and-forth exchanges.
ADVICE?	No	No advice.
ADMONISHMENTS?	No	No admonishments.
APOLOGIES?	No	No apologies.

IS IT A BIFF? YES

By replying to a stressed client's email with a BIFF, you help the client feel connected and reassured about the issue, without taking much of your time at all. This may also reduce the number of future contacts from the client simply for reassurance. High-conflict clients are especially anxious. Keeping things light and brief (rather than venting at the client for being a nuisance) will stabilize your relationship so you can focus more on the legal work in the long run.

Some of the hardest times for lawyers occur when their actions in the case have failed to help or have made things worse for their client. At times like these, how the lawyer handles the client's anger can make the difference between being sued and the client simply putting the issue behind them and focusing on what to do next. Perhaps ten percent of lawyers get sued each year, and many get sued at least once during their career. However, most of these lawsuits may actually be frivolous and unsuccessful, brought by disgruntled clients and based on poor communication by the lawyer rather than true attorney malpractice. Therefore, it's worth spending a few extra minutes forming a good BIFF Response when something goes wrong.

Confidential Information Released

From: Susan Condon (client)
To: James Rouse (attorney)
Subject: Email sent to my partner

Hi Jim,

I can't tell you how furious I am that you released a confidential communication of ours to the other side a month ago in my case! In it I confidentially told you that my former business partner was an a—hole and it has created more conflict between us in winding down our business partnership. On top of that, you have not responded to my many phone calls to discuss this for a whole month. I am on the verge of suing you for this and have an appointment scheduled with a LEGAL MALPRACTICE ATTORNEY. Will that be necessary to get you to talk to me???

Sue

Response 1

From: James Rouse
To: Susan Condon
Subject: RE: Email sent to my partner

Dear Susan,

There is nothing happening in your case right now, so there is nothing to discuss. Yes, it was unfortunate that our confidential communication was released to the other side a month ago, but no harm was caused by it. It's not legally relevant to any of the decisions that were made in the case. There is no basis for you to pursue a malpractice attorney—you're just wasting your own time and money.

I'll let you know when there is more work to do on finalizing your case.

Best regards,

Jim

BIFF CHECKER: YES OR NO

IS A RESPONSE NECESSARY?	Yes	The client is on the verge of suing the lawyer, so it would be wise to respond—especially since he hasn't communicated in a month!
BRIEF? (2 to 5 sentences)	Yes	It is a brief response; just a paragraph.
INFORMATIVE? (who, what, when, where, what for)	No	It's primarily dismissive and criticizing. Yes, he informs her there is no basis for a lawsuit, but it's defensive rather than explanatory.
FRIENDLY?	No	There are no friendly words.

FIRM?	Yes	The response is firm in that it is intended to end the angry conversation. However, it is quite dismissive and may inspire a further angry response.
ADVICE?	Yes	The lawyer states that the error was legally insignificant.
ADMONISHMENTS?	Yes	The lawyer is condescending in dismissing the client's concerns about the confidentiality error and admonishes her to forget about it.
APOLOGIES?	No	The attorney does not apologize for the error, though he unnecessarily dismisses it as insignificant.

IS IT A BIFF? NO

Response 2

From: James Rouse
To: Susan Condon
Subject: RE: Email sent to my partner

Dear Susan,

Thank you for reaching out to me and explaining your concerns. Let's set up a time to get together this week. I am still waiting for word from the other side for us to proceed with finalizing your case. I'll let you know when we are ready to do the paperwork for that.

I look forward to helping you wrap up this chapter of your life.

Best regards,

Jim

BIFF CHECKER: YES OR NO

IS A RESPONSE NECESSARY?	Yes	The client is on the verge of suing the lawyer, so it would be wise to respond.
BRIEF? (2 to 5 sentences)	Yes	It is brief; just five sentences.
INFORMATIVE? (who, what, when, where, what for)	Yes	The attorney says he would like to meet and also says he is waiting for word from the other side. No unnecessary comments are made.
FRIENDLY?	Yes	He thanks her for sharing her concerns and initiates a meeting, which is what she wanted. He indicates his desire to help her by wrapping this up.
FIRM?	Yes	He doesn't raise any issues that would hook her back in. He doesn't address her complaints directly, but because he sets up a meeting, it's not an obvious absence. They can discuss the confidentiality issue when they meet.
ADVICE?	No	No advice.
ADMONISHMENTS?	No	No admonishments.
APOLOGIES?	No	No apologies.

IS IT A BIFF? YES

It may seem like a glaring omission for him not to apologize for the breach of confidentiality, but doing so might reinforce a client's all-or-nothing thinking and open him up for a lawsuit. With potentially high-conflict people, apologizing often empowers them to take more aggressive action against you, not less. They can show the world that you admitted to an ethical mistake. It may be better to express regrets about it in person rather than in writing that can be brought up against the lawyer at any time for any purpose.

Wrongful Death?[7]

Ms. Constance Kapar, Attorney at Law:

Thank you for taking time to read my letter. I know you've said that the case is over and there's nothing else you can do to help me, but I can't stop thinking about it, especially the major mistake made in negotiations. We never should have conceded on giving the neighbors healthcare power of attorney over my Uncle Ben. When they approved the surgery that caused his death, I truly believe they killed him. They should not have pressured him. He was so old and trusting. I can't stop wondering why you, as an attorney who specializes in elder law, allowed this to happen; why you advised me to accept their proposal.

The more I think about it, I've truly begun to wonder if there was something going on behind the scenes. I know you and my uncle and the neighbors live in the same small town, so it makes sense that you know each other. Some online searching shows that you attend the same church, so now I'm really suspicious and feeling like the $25K I paid in legal fees, only to end up losing my uncle, was a complete waste. You must have known all along that you were going to persuade me to let them have the healthcare power of attorney.

I'm at a complete loss. I would like my money back. If you don't agree, I've decided to explore my options with another attorney, with the state bar complaints area, and even with law enforcement. Please send the refund to me at this address.

Sincerely,

Serena McCrory

---

7 This example first appeared in *BIFF at Work* by Bill Eddy and Megan Hunter (2021), Scottsdale, AZ: Unhooked Books, 72–75, titled: "Death of Uncle Ben."

Response 1

Dear Mrs. McCrory,

We were all deeply saddened by the passing of your Uncle Ben. But at his age and in his condition, surgery always carries a risk to it. Please understand that if he didn't get the surgery, there was also a risk of death. I'm attaching a copy of the letter from his doctor, who said it was about a 50-50 chance of him dying with or without the surgery. I don't remember if you ever saw this letter before, but he sent it to the neighbors before they approved the surgery.

I am disturbed that you imply in your letter that I somehow conspired with his neighbors to swing the healthcare power of attorney over to them. I did no such thing! I am, and have always been, a highly ethical lawyer, and I will challenge any attempts you make to tarnish my reputation. You are right that this is a small town, but I have an ethical duty to represent you, my client, without any conflict of interest. I believe I properly represented you, and you will not be receiving any refund. I worked tirelessly on your case, and any implication that I benefitted financially from your wealthy uncle's death is patently absurd.

Constance Kapar

Attorney at Law

BIFF CHECKER: YES OR NO

IS A RESPONSE NECESSARY?	Yes	Mrs. McCrory is an existing client.
BRIEF? (2 to 5 sentences)	No	At two full paragraphs, the response is not brief.

INFORMATIVE? (who, what, when, where, what for)	Yes and No	At first, it focuses on the reality of the risks, and a relevant letter is attached. But then it becomes very emotional and defensive. It even suggests that Ms. Kapar benefitted financially from Uncle Ben's death, a possibility that Mrs. McCrory herself never brought up or suggested. This raises a very concerning new question in the reader's mind: Did Ms. Kapar benefit?
FRIENDLY?	Yes and No	The first paragraph is relatively friendly, but the second paragraph erases that with its defensiveness.
FIRM?	Yes	Ms. Kapar is firm in her refusal to give a refund. However, her defensiveness is less likely to intimidate Mrs. McCrory and more likely to inspire her to investigate. The idea that the lawyer may have benefitted financially is now a new reason for her high-conflict client to look deeper.
ADVICE?	No	No advice.
ADMONISHMENTS?	Yes	This statement definitely feels like an admonishment: "I will challenge any attempts you make to tarnish my reputation."
APOLOGIES?	No	No apologies.

IS IT A BIFF? NO

Response 2

Dear Mrs. McCrory,

We were all deeply saddened by the passing of your Uncle Ben. At his age and in his condition, surgery always carries a risk to it. Please understand that if he didn't get the surgery, there was also a risk of death. I'm attaching a copy of the letter from his doctor, who said it was about a 50-50 chance of him dying with or without the surgery. I don't remember if you ever saw this letter before, but he sent it to the neighbors before they approved the surgery.

I hope this helps give you some peace that neither you nor I nor the neighbors did anything improper.

Very truly yours,

Constance Kapar

Attorney at Law

BIFF CHECKER: YES OR NO

IS A RESPONSE NECESSARY?	Yes	Mrs. McCrory is an existing client.
BRIEF? (2 to 5 sentences)	Yes	It's just six sentences.
INFORMATIVE? (who, what, when, where, what for)	Yes	It focuses on the reality of the risks. A relevant letter is attached, and that's it.
FRIENDLY?	Yes	The first paragraph shows some empathy, and the last sentence seeks to give the client peace of mind.
FIRM?	Yes	Although it doesn't address the refund issue directly, the rest of the letter strongly implies the answer by saying that no one did nothing wrong. (See chapter 10 for a discussion of refunds.)
ADVICE?	No	No advice.
ADMONISHMENTS?	No	No admonishments.
APOLOGIES?	No	No apologies.

IS IT A BIFF? YES

Conclusion

Clients' anxiety and stress can lead to tense communications even under the best of circumstances. When the client is a high-conflict person, this becomes even more likely. And when an attorney has made significant error or ethical lapse, it can become a major problem. By communicating well, quickly, and with empathy, a lawyer may avoid being sued and may help find a positive result for the client regardless of his mistake. A BIFF can go a long way in calming this type of situation.

CHAPTER 5

Initiating Difficult Issues with a Client

You can use the same BIFF format when initiating a written conversation, not just in response to a written communication. The message may need to be a little longer, so that you can explain the new topic. But don't say any more than is necessary, otherwise you may trigger an emotional disturbance in your client and have to spend more time calming things down again.

It can be especially helpful to write a follow-up email or letter after a meeting or conversation with the client that may be misunderstood or overwhelming. High-conflict clients often distort what they have heard to fit what they wanted to hear or what they were afraid that they heard. For example, one client had a hard time hearing the word "No." She recalled conversations as the attorney saying he or she *would* do something when the attorney had said they would *not* do that.

Requesting Records

Initial Email 1

From: Samira Ali (attorney)
To: Joshua Jackson (client)
Subject: Preparations for Court

Dear Mr. Jackson,

I am following up on our phone conversation. Your criminal trial is coming up soon, and I need several pieces of information from you ASAP:

Any prior arrests or convictions, and related paperwork. **This includes any state.** I know that you have been hiding them from me.

Any prior hospitalizations and related paperwork. **This includes any state.** I really need this because the other side will bring them up and I need to prepare a response.

Any prior lawsuits filed against you and related paperwork, whether they were dropped or a decision was made. **This includes any state.** Please don't try to avoid letting me know this information. The other side will find it and surprise us with it if you haven't told me in advance.

Up to now you have been a difficult client, and you need to start cooperating with me. You need to wake up and understand that you are in a desperate situation.

Very truly yours,

Samira Ali
Attorney at Law

BIFF CHECKER: YES OR NO

IS THIS COMMUNICATION NECESSARY?	Yes	The trial is coming soon, and the lawyer needs this information in order to adequately prepare.
BRIEF? (2 to 5 sentences)	Yes	It is longer than an ideal BIFF *Response* but relatively brief for *initiating* a request for specific information.

INFORMATIVE? (who, what, when, where, what for)	Yes	It does ask for specific information. However, it's also unnecessarily argumentative and insulting.
FRIENDLY?	No	There are no friendly words.
FIRM?	Yes	This email is firm. However, it will likely inspire a negative response, since the client may feel compelled to defend his actions and inactions.
ADVICE?	Yes	The lawyer advises her client to accept that he is in a bad position and start cooperating.
ADMONISHMENTS?	Yes	The lawyer is openly frustrated and admonishes the client about being uncooperative.
APOLOGIES?	No	No apologies.

IS IT A BIFF? NO

This initial draft includes some tempting admonishments, but it is a good example of what not to do in order to motivate a client. Criticisms and insults tend to provoke high-conflict clients to become more defensive and act worse, not better. It also doesn't help to "suggest the negative" by saying what you don't want ("Don't try to avoid letting me know this"). It's always best—especially with difficult clients—to speak in positive terms about what you *want* them to do rather than say what you *don't* want them to do. They can be very suggestible, so suggest the positive behavior. Also, avoid using bold formatting unless truly necessary. In this case, make it matter-of-fact by not using bold. Otherwise, it adds to the feeling of confrontation rather than being helpful.

Initial Email 2

From: Samira Ali (attorney)
To: Joshua Jackson (client)
Subject: Preparations for Court

Dear Mr. Jackson,

I am following up on our phone conversation. Your criminal trial is coming up soon, and I need several pieces of information from you. I understand it may be uncomfortable to tell me these things, but it is better that they come from you so we can prepare, rather than hearing it first from the other side during the trial. Please tell me of:

Any prior arrests or convictions, and related paperwork. This includes any state.

Any prior hospitalizations and related paperwork. This includes any state.

Any prior lawsuits filed against you and related paperwork, whether they were dismissed or a decision was made. This includes any state.

Let me know if you have questions about any of this. If possible, send me this information within the next seven days. I want us to be well prepared for your trial.

Very truly yours,

Samira Ali
Attorney at Law

BIFF CHECKER: YES OR NO

IS THIS COMMUNICATION NECESSARY?	Yes	The trial is coming soon, and the lawyer needs this information in order to adequately prepare.
BRIEF? (2 to 5 sentences)	Yes	It is longer than an ideal BIFF *Response* but relatively brief for *initiating* a request for specific information.
INFORMATIVE? (who, what, when, where, what for)	Yes	It asks for specific information and explains why it is needed, without becoming argumentative or insulting.
FRIENDLY?	Yes	The lawyer acknowledges that it may be uncomfortable for her client to share this information. She emphasizes the benefit of them being prepared, rather than suggesting the negative consequence if they are not.
FIRM?	Yes	The message is firm, yet there are no emotional hooks to encourage conflict about this.
ADVICE?	No	No advice.
ADMONISHMENTS?	No	Although the lawyer is frustrated, she avoids making any admonishments, knowing they would just make the situation worse.
APOLOGIES?	No	No apologies.

IS IT A BIFF? YES

You can hear the difference in tone of voice between the first and second drafts. By being matter-of-fact in the second draft, the lawyer avoids doing anything to trigger the client's defensiveness. Ironically, many lawyers try to motivate their high-conflict clients by admonishing and insulting them, but that doesn't work with HCPs. It's best to steer clear of negativity entirely.

Possible Termination

Initial Email 1

From: Emma Striker (attorney)
To: Jane Davis (client)
Subject: Disclosures

Dear Ms. Davis,

As you know, we need to submit your Financial Declarations soon to your husband's lawyer, and he will be sending us his. You have informed me that you will not disclose the jewelry that you own that is stored at your mother's house in another country, since you say it is your separate property. I have informed you that you MUST disclose this in order to have made a full and proper submission to the other side and to the court. Even though separate property is usually awarded to the individual who acquired it from a separate property source, it must be disclosed so your husband can ask any questions about the source of the funds for acquiring that separate property.

With this in mind, I must inform you that I cannot submit your Financial Declarations without this information. So, please include it when you fill out the attached form. Otherwise, it would be unethical for me and could put me in hot water with the court and the state bar association. Therefore, you must include this information so I can submit it to the other lawyer and to the court. If you don't, I will not be able to represent you and must withdraw from your case. You have seven days to provide me this full information when you return this form, or I will withdraw.

Regards,
Emma Striker

BIFF CHECKER: YES OR NO

IS THIS COMMUNICATION NECESSARY?	Yes	There is a problem with the client's resistance to doing the required disclosures, so the lawyer must address it. Of course, it is a judgment call whether it would be preferable to do this in a conversation.
BRIEF? (2 to 5 sentences)	No	An initial BIFF communication is often longer than a BIFF *Response*, because you have to explain more, but this is longer than necessary.
INFORMATIVE? (who, what, when, where, what for)	Yes	It asks for specific information and explains why. However, it ends with an unnecessary threat.
FRIENDLY?	No	There are no friendly words.
FIRM?	Yes	The lawyer informs her client that she must provide the information so it can be disclosed. However, this email will likely inspire a negative response, since it unnecessarily suggests the negative ("If you don't...") and then threatens to end the attorney-client relationship.
ADVICE?	No	No advice.
ADMONISHMENTS?	No	No, not talking down to or insulting client.
APOLOGIES?	No	No apologies.

IS IT A BIFF? NO

At first, this might seem like a reasonable and necessary email, given the client's resistance already. However, since this is the first written communication on this topic, it's best to make it totally positive and explanatory, without including negatives. If there is a bad response to the first written communication, then in the follow-up communication the lawyer can explain that the client's choices will have consequences. But start out on a positive foot.

Initial Email 2

From: Emma Striker (attorney)
To: Jane Davis (client)
Subject: Disclosures

Dear Ms. Davis,

As you know, we need to submit your Financial Declarations soon to your husband's lawyer, and he will be sending us his. While you initially informed me that you will not disclose all your jewelry, you need to include it even if it's in another country. The law says separate as well as community property must be disclosed so your husband can ask any questions about the source of funds for acquiring that separate property. Don't worry; if it clearly came from a separate source, it will be assigned to you in full. It's just a procedural matter.

So, please send me all your property information in all the categories in the attached form in the next seven days, so I can prepare the Financial Disclosure.

Let me know if you have any questions. I look forward to helping you put all of this behind you soon.

Thanks,
Emma Striker

BIFF CHECKER: YES OR NO

IS THIS COMMUNICATION NECESSARY?	Yes	There is a problem with the client's resistance to doing the required disclosures, so the lawyer must address it. Of course, it is a judgment call whether it would be preferable to do this in a conversation.
BRIEF? (2 to 5 sentences)	Yes	An initial BIFF communication is often longer than a BIFF *Response*, but this is only eight sentences, which seems reasonable.
INFORMATIVE? (who, what, when, where, what for)	Yes	It carefully informs the client of what is necessary, in a totally positive manner without any negative words. It creates an expectation that she will, of course, provide all of the necessary information.
FRIENDLY?	Yes	The lawyer seeks to put her client's mind at ease and says she wants to help put this behind her.
FIRM?	Yes	It ends the discussion of the issue. By following this clear explanation with an offer to answer any questions, she makes the message feel less threatening or forceful.
ADVICE?	No	No advice.
ADMONISHMENTS?	No	No, not talking down to or insulting client.
APOLOGIES?	No	No apologies.

IS IT A BIFF? YES

The tone of this email is completely different and more likely to inspire cooperation. But suppose the client still refuses to include the separate jewelry and says so in another email or text. Here's a possible BIFF Response.

Response to Negative Client Reply

From: Emma Striker (attorney)
To: Jane Davis (client)
Subject: RE: Disclosures

Dear Ms. Davis,

I was saddened to receive your reply. I should let you know that not including all assets I know about would be unethical for me and could put me in hot water with the court and the state bar association. Therefore, you must include this information. If you don't, I will unfortunately not be able to represent you. Now is actually a good time for us to go separate ways, if necessary, because no hearings or trials have been scheduled. I hope this won't be necessary. The choice is up to you but must be made in the next five days so I can prepare the form for you.

Best wishes,

Emma Striker

BIFF CHECKER: YES OR NO

IS THIS COMMUNICATION NECESSARY?	Yes	A lawyer should almost always respond to a client's email. Of course, a phone call might be a better way to respond, although this email appears appropriate.
BRIEF? (2 to 5 sentences)	Yes	It's brief enough while including important information.
INFORMATIVE? (who, what, when, where, what for)	Yes	It informs the client of the ethics issue and the possibility of termination, without blaming anyone.

FRIENDLY?	Yes	The lawyer gives a friendly tone to this difficult message by saying "I hope this won't be necessary" and "It's up to you."
FIRM?	Yes	It needs a response, and it narrows it to two choices and gives a deadline.
ADVICE?	No	No advice.
ADMONISHMENTS?	No	No, not talking down to or insulting client.
APOLOGIES?	No	No apologies.

IS IT A BIFF? YES

Conclusion

These are good examples of a lawyer initiating new topics with a client in the BIFF format. BIFF works just as well in starting a conversation as it does in response to a client's communication, and it may avoid triggering any hostility for the whole discussion. Remember, high-conflict people are very suggestible, so don't "suggest the negative."

This chapter also shows how a lawyer can respond to the client's reply to their initial email or letter. By saving the negative information and tough choices for the follow-up communication, the lawyer can keep the initial communication totally positive and relatively brief. If it works, another email may not be necessary.

CHAPTER 6

Communicating with Family Members of a Client

Family members (and friends, coworkers, and neighbors) are often involved in the legal matters of clients, especially if the client has a high-conflict personality. Some easily become negative advocates, who have absorbed the client's high-conflict thinking and feelings, and who defend their actions—as extreme as they may be. Others can be helpful and positive, at times calming an upset client or providing useful information and resources. Of course, ordinary clients may also have family members involved for various reasons, including helping to pay your fees.

Therefore, it is wise to respond to written communications from such family members, both to help them calm down and to maintain good client relations. However, it is always best to discuss such communications with your client first, so you know their relationship with the person. Sometimes, your client may not want you to respond, and other times they may be too eager to involve the family member. So, communicating with the family member offers you the opportunity to help manage both the client and the family member.

Complaint from Client's Wife

From: Saman Killian (client's wife)
To: Jasper Rouhani (attorney)
Subject: Need Updates

Hello Mr. Rouhani,

I am Thomas Killian's wife, and you have represented my husband for the past year. I have heard complaints from Thomas that you take weeks to respond, and this is unacceptable. As his attorney, you have a duty to respond in a timely manner. Thomas is currently in immigration proceedings, which is very stressful for us. I am also pregnant with our third child, and we do not need this extra stress. Thomas needs to know the status of his case, and we need a timely response so we can plan appropriately for his hearing. We have two young children, and we both have full-time jobs. This is just one more stressor in our lives. Thomas and I are at wit's end and need responses in a timely manner.

We will have to end this relationship if things do not change!

Sincerely,
Saman

Response 1

From: Jasper Rouhani (attorney)
To: Saman Killian (client's wife)
Subject: RE: Need Updates

Hello Ms. Killian,

I have been in touch with your husband, and we are in communication. I do not appreciate your message reprimanding me. My client is your husband, and I will continue to communicate with him only.

Thank you,

Jasper

BIFF CHECKER: YES OR NO

IS A RESPONSE NECESSARY?	Yes	Generally, yes, but the lawyer should check with the client first. He may have encouraged this communication from his wife, or he may think that she is meddling and not want you to respond.
BRIEF? (2 to 5 sentences)	Yes	Very brief and to the point.
INFORMATIVE? (who, what, when, where, what for)	Yes	It clarifies that the attorney is already in contact with his client, but it adds unnecessary hostility.
FRIENDLY?	No	The overall tone of the email is not friendly. The attorney is defensive and cuts off communication with his client's wife.
FIRM?	Yes	Yes, this is a firm response in that it ends the hostile communication.
ADVICE?	No	No advice.
ADMONISHMENTS?	Yes	The attorney admonishes his client's wife for contacting him. This might be an appropriate message, but the way he states it is unfriendly.
APOLOGIES?	No	No apologies.

IS IT A BIFF? NO

Response 2

From: Jasper Rouhani (attorney)
To: Saman Killian (client's wife)
Subject: RE: Need Updates

Hello Ms. Killian,

I understand that you are frustrated with the immigration process. Things tend to move very slowly in immigration court. I have been in contact with your husband and told him I would reach out when I have an update.

I am happy to CC you on those updates, with your husband's permission. I hope that helps.

Thank you, and I will contact you as soon as I hear anything from the court.

Best regards,
Jasper

BIFF CHECKER: YES OR NO

IS A RESPONSE NECESSARY?	Yes	Responding is generally a good idea, especially with an upset family member, provided the client agrees.
BRIEF? (2 to 5 sentences)	Yes	Brief and to the point.
INFORMATIVE? (who, what, when, where, what for)	Yes	The attorney provides a concrete picture of the process and helps his client's wife understand the next steps. He also offers to keep her in the loop with his client's permission.
FRIENDLY?	Yes	The email is very friendly and understanding.
FIRM?	Yes	The attorney acknowledges the frustration expressed in the initial email but remains firm and focused on future-facing solutions.
ADVICE?	No	No advice.
ADMONISHMENTS?	No	No admonishments.
APOLOGIES?	No	Rather than apologizing, the attorney acknowledges the negative emotions being expressed and describes the source of the delay, which in this case is the immigration court.

IS IT A BIFF? YES

The Angry Daughter

From: Michelle Diop (client's daughter)
To: Raya Khan (attorney)
Subject: Problems with affidavit

Hello Ms. Khan,

I am David Diop's daughter. You have been representing my father in his immigration proceedings for the past year. He is very unhappy with your representation, and I agree. I read the affidavit you drafted. There are clearly language issues here, and you misrepresented my father and his journey to the United States. My father explicitly stated that the most difficult part of his journey to the United States was when he had to fly to Mexico first and enter the United States from there. You did not include this in his affidavit. This makes me very concerned that you have left out other crucial details from his affidavit. This is my father's one chance in court, and it is extremely important that we get it right.

I have taken a hands-off approach in this case out of respect to my father, but now I believe I must interfere. We will have to look for another attorney if this is not corrected right away! We need to have another meeting with you, me, and my father. We will also need an interpreter present to make sure everything is recorded.

Michelle

Response 1

From: Raya Khan (attorney)
To: Michelle Diop (client's daughter)
Subject: RE: Problems with affidavit

Hello Michelle,

I understand that you are upset, but I have been working hard on your father's case for the past year. I apologize that the affidavit is not as accurate as you would like. I have been using a French interpreter with your father so that I can get everything as accurate as possible. Your father has never expressed any issues, and I am confused as to why you are speaking on his behalf now.

Please tell your father to contact me.

Thanks,
Raya, Esq.

BIFF CHECKER: YES OR NO

IS A RESPONSE NECESSARY?	Yes	After checking with the client, it's generally good to respond to an upset family member.
BRIEF? (2 to 5 sentences)	Yes	Brief, though not to the point.
INFORMATIVE? (who, what, when, where, what for)	Yes	The email does explain the situation, but there is also a lot of other unnecessary information. Furthermore, email may not be the best format to discuss the issue.
FRIENDLY?	No	Although there are elements that are friendly, the overall tone is aggressive. The attorney is annoyed that the client's daughter is interfering, and this energy comes through in the email.
FIRM?	No	Phrases like "I am confused as to why" leave the email too open ended. The attorney does not address the daughter's involvement in her father's case, which is allowed with the consent of the client.

ADVICE?	No	No advice.
ADMONISHMENTS?	Yes	She admonishes the client for criticizing her work and being involved in her client's case. The attorney is matching the daughter's energy, which is not helpful in this case.
APOLOGIES?	Yes	The attorney offers an apology and then undermines it with her later comments. The apology feels performative rather than sincere.

IS IT A BIFF? NO

Response 2

From: Raya Khan (attorney)
To: Michelle Diop (client's daughter)
Subject: RE: Problems with affidavit

Hello Ms. Diop,

I understand that you are frustrated, and I would be happy to discuss the affidavit with you and your father. We are still two months away from your father's hearing, so there is plenty of time to update and correct his affidavit.

Please let me know when you all are available next week to meet in person.

Thank you,
Raya, Esq.

BIFF CHECKER: YES OR NO

IS A RESPONSE NECESSARY?	Yes	After checking with client, it's generally good to respond to an upset family member.
BRIEF? (2 to 5 sentences)	Yes	Brief and to the point.
INFORMATIVE? (who, what, when, where, what for)	Yes	The attorney addresses all the key points the client's daughter mentioned. The message is constructive and informative; it focuses on future-facing problem solving.
FRIENDLY?	Yes	The attorney acknowledges the daughter's frustration. The email is friendly and sets the tone for future interactions with the daughter and her father.
FIRM?	Yes	The attorney asks for a concrete response about meeting next week.
ADVICE?	No	No advice.
ADMONISHMENTS?	No	No admonishments. The attorney does not match the daughter's energy and rather de-escalates and neutralizes the whole interaction. This will be useful for when they meet in person.
APOLOGIES?	No	No apologies.

IS IT A BIFF? YES

Conclusion

The examples in this chapter address situations that commonly occur with family members. Often, this type of negative feedback may come in a phone call, and in this case the same basic approach can be used: be brief, informative, friendly, and firm.

An important point in all communications from family members is that you check with your client before you respond. In high-conflict families, there often are weak boundaries (family members are highly involved and meddling) or extreme boundaries (you will not be allowed to communicate with family members at all).

While family members can pose some challenges, they can also be very helpful in managing an upset or difficult client. Your communication with them may help you resolve your case. Communicating over the phone or in person is often a good idea if you don't want comments in writing to be taken the wrong way. Verbally using the BIFF method can help in these sticky family situations.

CHAPTER 7

Communicating with a Nonresponsive Client

Clients can be nonresponsive for many reasons, including technical email and phone difficulties, being in the midst of moving, and having overwhelming responsibilities in a difficult time (with their job, kids, and so on). However, high-conflict clients can also fail to respond for absurd reasons having to do with their difficult personalities.

Bill had one client who flat-out told him: "Why didn't I respond to your letter? Don't you know that I put all of the mail I get from you in a separate pile? A pile of mail I don't open because it's too upsetting!" The letter contained a reasonable settlement proposal from the other lawyer that she needed to review and approve, at which point her case would be over. Talk about all-or-nothing thinking!

Even if the ball is clearly in your client's court and you are frustrated by their unresponsiveness, we suggest that you reach out to them. You can do this by making a phone call, with a follow-up email; or by sending an email with a follow-up phone call. Different people communicate more easily or often using one method or another. It's tempting to be insistent and threatening, but generally the best approach seems to be staying reasonable, using the BIFF method, and following up persistently. This is what attorney Asher Conway did, when her phone message got a minimal response from her client.

Procrastinating Client

From: Katie Wu (client)
To: Asher Conway (attorney)
Subject: Got your message

Hello Asher,

I received your message. I will respond next week.

Thanks,

Katie

Response 1

From: Asher Conway (attorney)
To: Katie Wu (client)
Subject: RE: Got your message

Hello Katie,

I have been trying to reach you for two weeks. I need your statement ASAP. We have to be in court in two weeks, and I can't submit your materials without your affidavit. I EXPLICITLY stated in the retainer that you signed that there would be client-attorney cooperation. That standard is clearly not being met here. This is my last attempt to schedule an appointment with you, or we will have to discuss termination.

Best,

Asher

BIFF CHECKER: YES OR NO

IS A RESPONSE NECESSARY?	Yes	The attorney needs to prepare an affidavit. While this might be better handled in a phone call, the client has already not responded to a phone call.
BRIEF? (2 to 5 sentences)	Yes	The email is brief, though there is extra unnecessary information.
INFORMATIVE? (who, what, when, where, what for)	Yes	The email does remind the client of her responsibilities. However, it does so condescendingly and angrily, so the important information will likely get lost.
FRIENDLY?	No	The attorney's frustration comes through in the email's angry and hostile tone.
FIRM?	No	There is too much rambling and unnecessary information for the email to be firm. It might end the conversation, but the lawyer is seeking a response.
ADVICE?	No	No advice.
ADMONISHMENTS?	Yes	There are admonishments for the client's lack of communication. Although the attorney has every right to be frustrated, this is not the best way to handle the situation.
APOLOGIES?	No	No apologies.

IS IT A BIFF? NO

Response 2

From: Asher Conway (attorney)
To: Katie Wu (client)
Subject: For Your Immediate Review

Hello Katie,

Thank you for letting me know you received my message. I am in the process of submitting your filing to the court, and I still need to complete your affidavit with you. If we cannot do so in the next week, this will delay your case further.

Please call me in the next three days to set up an appointment. We will have to discuss alternative arrangements if we cannot complete the affidavit within the week.

I look forward to hearing from you.

Best,

Asher

BIFF CHECKER: YES OR NO

IS A RESPONSE NECESSARY?	Yes	The attorney needs to submit the affidavit.
BRIEF? (2 to 5 sentences)	Yes	The email is just a few sentences.
INFORMATIVE? (who, what, when, where, what for)	Yes	The attorney explains what must be completed and provides concrete deadlines.
FRIENDLY?	Yes	The email is very friendly and expresses concern over the matter. The attorney is likely still frustrated, but he provides concrete next steps that the client can follow or not.
FIRM?	Yes	The response is firm and does not dilute its message with unnecessary information. The attorney could have provided specific details about the retainer agreement and client obligations, but this was not necessary for a firm response.

ADVICE?	No	No advice.
ADMONISHMENTS?	No	No admonishments. Instead, the attorney lays out a clear plan moving forward.
APOLOGIES?	No	No apologies.

IS IT A BIFF? YES

Nonresponsive Client

This client has not been responding to any of his attorney's calls or emails.

Response 1

From: Zamia Johnson (attorney)
To: Tahir Wade (client)
Subject: FINAL NOTICE

Hello Tahir,

I have called and emailed you for over two weeks. YOU NEED TO RESPOND. We are supposed to go to court next week!!

If you do not respond by tomorrow, I will submit a Motion to Withdraw from our professional relationship!

Zamia

BIFF CHECKER: YES OR NO

IS A RESPONSE NECESSARY?	Yes	Action is needed because the trial is coming up.
BRIEF? (2 to 5 sentences)	Yes	The email is brief.

INFORMATIVE? (who, what, when, where, what for)	Yes	It is informative and states the consequences of a client not returning an attorney's calls.
FRIENDLY?	No	The tone is hostile and tense. It is understandable that the attorney is so upset, but the way she is wording her message will likely not help with getting a reply from the client.
FIRM?	No	Although this message sounds firm, it leaves too much room for a defensive response.
ADVICE?	No	No advice.
ADMONISHMENTS?	Yes	The attorney is clearly angry, and the entire email is basically an admonishment.
APOLOGIES?	No	No apologies.

IS IT A BIFF? NO

Response 2

From: Zamia Johnson (attorney)
To: Tahir Wade (client)
Subject: Time Sensitive Response

Hello Tahir,

We have an upcoming court date next week. As stated in your retainer, I can provide services only if there is cooperation and a working relationship. If I am not able to get hold of you this week, unfortunately, I will have to progress with terminating our professional relationship. I hope that won't be necessary.

Please let me know how you would like to move forward.

Thank you,
Zamia

BIFF CHECKER: YES OR NO

IS A RESPONSE NECESSARY?	Yes	Action needed because the trial is coming up.
BRIEF? (2 to 5 sentences)	Yes	The attorney states only what is necessary and is concise in laying out the next steps.
INFORMATIVE? (who, what, when, where, what for)	Yes	The attorney has clearly done her best to get in touch with her client and now has created a clear path forward.
FRIENDLY?	Yes	The tone is stern but still neutral. This is a very serious matter, and there is no way around that. Given the circumstances, the attorney remains relatively calm and friendly.
FIRM?	Yes	The attorney makes it clear that in order for them to continue their relationship, the client must reach out. The attorney also discusses the limits that she set in the retainer regarding cooperation and communication for adequate legal representation.
ADVICE?	No	No advice.
ADMONISHMENTS?	No	No admonishments. The attorney is frustrated; anyone would be in this situation. But the attorney approaches this graciously and offers to continue the working relationship.
APOLOGIES?	No	No apologies.

IS IT A BIFF? YES

Conclusion

Nonresponsive clients should be anticipated in today's world of uncommunicative people. Have a system in place for such situations, and explain it from the start of your work with clients so they know what to expect if they don't respond. You can say something like this:

> "Some clients don't respond in a timely matter to important communications. You probably won't be like that, but in order for me to help you, we need to have close communication. Can you agree that you will respond to emails, voicemails, and letters within three days of receipt?"
>
> [Clients usually say yes at the start of working together.]
>
> "That's great, and I will make every effort to do the same."

Later, if you have to send a BIFF about a late response, you can always refer to this message as a gentle reminder.

CHAPTER 8

Terminating a Relationship with a Client

Always be prepared for the need to terminate with a client, either because the client fails to respond or to pay for services, or because you determine that you can no longer work with a client now that the case (or client) has come into focus as beyond your abilities. Whatever the reason, it is wise to refrain from blaming the client ("You are an irresponsible person") or blaming yourself ("I was not the right attorney for your case").

Either one of these comments may trigger a high-conflict client to take action against you, because you blamed ("abandoned") them or you should have known better than to take their case in the first place if you weren't "qualified" to handle it. In either case, they may consider suing you or demand money back. (Sometimes money back is a good idea, as we'll discuss in chapter 10.)

If you decide to terminate with a client, keep the message neutral and emphasize that your goals or approaches were different or that you just weren't a good fit with each other for some reason. It is also reasonable to refer to retainer agreements or some external agreement stating client responsibilities.

The following is an email composed after a brief phone call about termination with a client. A new client had left a vaguely threatening voicemail for the attorney about her not being assertive enough to file for an emergency hearing. This was over a minor matter, which made an emergency hearing inappropriate. The courts insist that emergency hearings are only used for true emergencies. The lawyer realized immediately that starting out the case this way was a warning sign that it was only likely to get worse. Since no hearings or trials were scheduled yet, it was a good time to get out. If it had been later in the case, the attorney might not have been able to exit so easily and might have had to file a Motion to Withdraw subject to the court's approval, which might not be given because the withdrawal would prejudice or delay the client's case.

The Sudden Termination

Draft Communication 1

From: Mary Weekly (attorney)
To: Joe Little (client)
Subject: Ending Representation

Dear Joe,

I wanted to follow up on our discussion about ending my representation of you in your case. It has become clear to me that you expect me to make your case the sole focus of my work, with constant court hearings over minor matters. I cannot tolerate that. I have many clients, and you cannot monopolize my time. It's time for us to go our separate ways. I have attached the form for you to sign to transfer me out of the case so that you can start with a new attorney. I can give you some suggestions or you can go to whomever you like.

Best wishes,
Mary Weekly

BIFF CHECKER: YES OR NO

IS A COMMUNICATION NECESSARY?	Yes	If Mary feels she cannot handle this client, it's better to get out sooner rather than later. Since they already had a conversation about this sensitive topic, a written communication is a good idea so the client is clear on what happened and doesn't distort or bad-mouth the lawyer to others in the community.
BRIEF? (2 to 5 sentences)	Yes	It's just a paragraph.
INFORMATIVE? (who, what, when, where, what for)	Yes	It makes clear that she wants to end the relationship, and she explains why, but this is a bad idea, as explained under Friendly.
FRIENDLY?	No	It's not at all friendly. While you might think it doesn't matter since they are going their separate ways, this can make the difference between being sued or bad-mouthed to the community—or not.
FIRM?	No	It is unnecessarily rejecting, which may trigger an angry response or lawsuit, less likely for malpractice.
ADVICE?	No	No advice.
ADMONISHMENTS?	Yes	She admonishes him for monopolizing her time, which is hostile and unnecessary at this point.
APOLOGIES?	No	No apologies.

IS IT A BIFF? NO

Draft Communication 2

From: Mary Weekly (attorney)
To: Joe Little (client)
Subject: Ending Representation

Dear Joe,

I wanted to follow up on our discussion about ending my representation in your case. As I mentioned, occasionally attorney and client have different goals or approaches to the case. In this case, you prefer to bring many matters to court, while I am moving in the other direction in my practice to handling matters primarily out of court. When there is a difference, it's optimal to find a better fit as soon as possible. There are many good litigation attorneys in town, and I can give you some names if you wish. I will be pleased to assist in providing case information to your new lawyer.

I have enclosed the form you will need your new attorney to sign to replace me. I will also refund your full retainer when I receive the signed form. Let me know if you have any questions. I wish you success in your case.

Best wishes,
Mary

BIFF CHECKER: YES OR NO

IS A COMMUNICATION NECESSARY?	Yes	If Mary feels she cannot handle this client, it's better to get out sooner rather than later. Since they already had a conversation about this sensitive topic, a written communication is a good idea so the client is clear on what happened and doesn't distort or bad-mouth the lawyer to others in the community.

BRIEF? (2 to 5 sentences)	Yes	Since this is an initial communication, it's a little longer than a BIFF *Response*. That is because there is more information to provide.
INFORMATIVE? (who, what, when, where, what for)	Yes	The email makes clear that this is not unusual and that they simply have different approaches, without blaming him or her. If someone else reads it, it sounds reasonable.
FRIENDLY?	Yes	It also sounds friendly. She's trying to be as helpful as she can under the circumstances.
FIRM?	Yes	Her explanations and determination essentially end discussion on the issue. If the client wants her to keep working for him, this email makes clear that this is not an option. She is firm in her decision.
ADVICE?	No	No advice.
ADMONISHMENTS?	No	No admonishments; she is very careful not to sound like she is blaming him for doing something wrong.
APOLOGIES?	No	No apologies.

IS IT A BIFF? YES

Conclusion

Termination is a very important and sensitive topic for lawyers and clients. Handling it skillfully has helped many lawyers gently remove themselves from potentially explosive cases and lawsuits from clients. No blame, no shame.

In this real case above, it was a wise move to refund the full retainer, because no substantive work had been done on the case at that point. The client found her own new lawyer, and they parted in peace.

CHAPTER 9

Website Contacts and Potential Client Inquiries

Websites are a modern reality. Because they are open to the world, they can bring in their share of hostile and misinformed communications, including from high-conflict people preoccupied with blaming lawyers and law offices. These people may have no interest in actually using and paying for your services, yet they may seek free information—a pursuit that can be endless, with question after question after question. Law offices need to develop policies about how they handle inquiries. By using the BIFF method, you and your staff can save time while responding respectfully.

Here's one example.

Website Blamespeak[8]

From: Jim Mendoza

After many years knowing and following your website and reading your content, I see your law firm as just more of your money grab under the guise of "helping." I'm on your site now and disappointed that because I'm using the contact form on this page, I can't add other people to this email. They need to know. Since you charge a fee, do you have any referrals to anyone who will collect their fees on performance rather than your

---

8 This example first appeared in *BIFF at Work* by Bill Eddy and Megan Hunter (2021), Scottsdale, AZ: Unhooked Books, 51–54.

"hourly" rate? I don't want the same old excuse that you can't give free "legal" advice, which to me seems like a way to avoid providing "actual" solutions. You and your entire industry continue harming and then just deny, deny, deny and collect, collect, collect $$$.

Response 1

Mr. Mendoza:

I'm so sorry to know that you feel this way about our law firm, and I hope you will reconsider your assessment. All of us work extraordinarily hard to provide a lot of helpful information and services at reasonable rates to anyone who visits our site (free) or calls our office (fee for service). As a business, we have to keep our doors open somehow, and therefore we charge for our services. While we wish we could help everyone for free, it's simply not realistic, and I truly hope you can understand this. We do "help" people. We do provide "actual" solutions. We do not give excuses. We do not harm, deny and collect $$$.

I don't know what profession you work in, but let me ask you this: Do you charge a fee for your services? I imagine you get paid for the work you do. Are you beginning to see where I'm going with this? I hope this gives you some insight into where we're coming from.

As to the contact form on the site, we are bound by the platform on which our website is built. It does not have the capability of copying in other people.

Please let me know if you have additional questions.

Sincerely,
Janna Walker

BIFF CHECKER: YES OR NO

IS A RESPONSE NECESSARY?	Yes	If the firm did not reply, the person could bad-mouth them for ignoring inquiries. A very brief BIFF is often the best approach.
BRIEF? (2 to 5 sentences)	No	The response goes too long and gives more information than is necessary— enough to irritate a potential client who has already shown himself to be angry.
INFORMATIVE? (who, what, when, where, what for)	Yes	It explains that the firm charges for services. But it also goes into justifying and defending, which often feeds more conflict.
FRIENDLY?	No	It makes an effort: "I hope you reconsider..."; "I hope this gives you some insight...." However, any genuine friendliness is undercut by "I don't know what profession you work in, but let me ask you this."
FIRM?	No	By encouraging more questions at the end, the email invites another angry response.
ADVICE?	No	Not really.
ADMONISHMENTS?	Yes	It feels a bit like an admonishment to explain and then say "I hope this gives you some insight," as if the person wasn't seeing the obvious before.
APOLOGIES?	Yes	It starts with "I'm so sorry you feel this way." While that isn't really an apology, it sounds like one because of the "sorry." It's better not to use that word at all, so doesn't imply an apology that isn't necessary and doesn't irritate a potential client because it sounds like an empty apology.

IS IT A BIFF? NO

Response 2

Hello Mr. Mendoza,

Thank you for your inquiry. We are a firm that provides legal services at reasonable rates. We have free educational articles on our website, but we do not offer free services and do not make referrals.

Best wishes,
Janna Walker

BIFF CHECKER: YES OR NO

IS A RESPONSE NECESSARY?	Yes	For good public relations.
BRIEF? (2 to 5 sentences)	Yes	This is brief and to the point.
INFORMATIVE? (who, what, when, where, what for)	Yes	This answers the potential client's questions and explains that there are free articles but no free services, and that it is not a law office, which appears to be what the person was seeking.
FRIENDLY?	Yes	There is a "thank you" opening and a "best wishes" closing.
FIRM?	Yes	It leaves no opening for further complaining, because it fully addresses what the potential client was looking for.
ADVICE?	No	No advice.
ADMONISHMENTS?	No	No admonishments.
APOLOGIES?	No	No apologies.

IS IT A BIFF? YES

Conclusion

This inquiry is an extreme example, but in today's world it's common that people publicly bash lawyers, and the Internet especially invites hostile and misinformed remarks, as well as public venting. It's best not to engage, and yet you can respectfully reply with a BIFF. That way the person who handles website information requests is less likely to get personally hooked or spend a lot of unnecessary time arguing with someone.

CHAPTER 10

Mediation Clients, Refund Issues, and Copying Issues

Many attorneys these days are also providing mediation services or representing clients in their mediation sessions. Mediators who handle divorce often meet with the parties without lawyers but refer their clients to consult with or retain lawyers with whom they communicate between sessions and who review their marital settlement agreements before the parties sign them. If you are involved in mediation, you may be faced with hostile or misinformed communication in this context.

The following example demonstrates how one experienced attorney-mediator handled a correspondence from a disgruntled mediation client. It also includes a lesson for anyone responding to a demand for a refund in any case and a lesson about whether to send a copy of your response to someone else.

Disgruntled Mediation Client

From: Joe Tarrant (mediation client)
To: Frank Perin (mediator)
Subject: Canceling

You met with us on Sept. 9th for our divorce mediation, and we scheduled another meeting for Sept. 23rd. We are now canceling that meeting, because both my wife and I (and my attorney) believe that you did not handle our mediation properly.

We accomplished nothing in our first meeting. I paid for the first mediation session, and I would like my money back. Please respond promptly. We have found another mediator who does it correctly.

Sincerely,
Joe Tarrant

The mediator was surprised. He'd never received such a letter before. He recalled that this was a client who came late, took calls on his cell phone, and made several blaming comments toward his wife during the session. No lawyers were present. The mediator was tempted to comment on the client's behavior in reply. However, he kept that out of his response.

Response 1

From: Frank Perin (mediator)
To: Joe Tarrant (mediation client)
Subject: RE: Canceling

Thank you for letting me know how upset you were about our mediation session and that you are cancelling the next session. Please read my policy that there are no refunds for services rendered. It's in my contract you signed. You should be attentive to what you sign and keep a copy.

Good luck with your new mediator.

Sincerely,
Frank Perin

BIFF CHECKER: YES OR NO

IS A RESPONSE NECESSARY?	Yes	If you don't respond to an angry client, you are likely to get an angrier response. Also, the client is likely to bad-mouth you online.
BRIEF? (2 to 5 sentences)	Yes	Just five sentences.
INFORMATIVE? (who, what, when, where, what for)	Yes	It informs the client there will be no refund according to the mediator's policy. However, it goes beyond that in an unnecessary way.
FRIENDLY?	No	The mediator thanks the client and wishes him good luck, but cancels out the positive with a negative comment.
FIRM?	No	Refunds are a touchy issue. While this response sounds firm, it is unlikely to end the hostile conversation. Not getting the refund and the "read the policy" comment are likely to trigger an angry response.
ADVICE?	No	No advice.
ADMONISHMENTS?	Yes	The mediator admonishes the client for not reading his policy about refunds. This is an insult likely to enrage him.
APOLOGIES?	No	No apologies.

IS IT A BIFF? NO

Response 2

From: Frank Perin (mediator)
To: Joe Tarrant (mediation client)
Subject: RE: Canceling

Dear Mr. Tarrant,

Thank you for your letter expressing your concerns about our mediation session. After doing nearly a thousand divorce mediation cases and teaching a course in mediation at two law schools, I have learned that people have different styles of providing mediation services. I am glad you have found a mediator who fits for you. Best wishes in completing your divorce.

Sincerely,
Frank Perin

BIFF CHECKER: YES OR NO

IS A RESPONSE NECESSARY?	Yes	If you don't respond to an angry client, you are likely to get an angrier response. Also, the client is likely to bad-mouth you online.
BRIEF? (2 to 5 sentences)	Yes	Just four sentences.
INFORMATIVE? (who, what, when, where, what for)	Maybe	It talks about the mediator's experience and explains that there are different styles. However, it doesn't answer the question of whether there will be a refund. Will this be a problem? See below.
FRIENDLY?	Yes	He thanks his client, says he's glad they found a mediator that fits, and wishes him well completing his divorce.
FIRM?	Maybe	Refunds are a touchy issue. It's not clear whether this response will be sufficient to end the hostile conversation. See below.
ADVICE?	No	No advice.
ADMONISHMENTS?	No	Not this time.
APOLOGIES?	No	No apologies.

IS IT A BIFF? MAYBE

Responding to a Refund Demand

This mediator's response to his client was a very reasonable first move. However, it wasn't exactly firm in that it did not respond to the client's request for a refund, leaving open the possibility of further conversation.

Why didn't the mediator tell the client directly that he would not refund his money? His reasoning was that he had performed his services satisfactorily and that explaining his experience sufficiently implied that he had not provided an inadequate service. He framed the issue as mediators having different styles, which was a gentle way of avoiding making it personal and saying how inappropriate the client's behavior was (including seeking a refund after such behavior). Since a sense of entitlement and lack of awareness of his own negative behavior is typical of high-conflict clients, it helps to be as brief as possible in responding and keep your reply relatively impersonal.

Also, the mediator didn't want to make the client *think* any further about a refund, since raising the issue and then rejecting it would have been likely to reinforce the client's negative mood. This BIFF seemed to be the approach least likely to trigger his defensiveness.

As it turned out, the mediator's intuition was correct; he never heard from the client again. The response appears to have helped the client let go. If the client had followed up with a more demanding correspondence, the mediator could have sent a BIFF responding firmly that he was not issuing a refund. But that turned out not to be necessary in this case.

This example demonstrates one way you might respond to an unjustified refund demand from a high-conflict client. However, there are some cases where you would be wise to respond by giving a refund, such as in the example in chapter 8, "Terminating a Relationship with a Client." In that situation, the client was requesting a refund before any substantive work had been done.

Should You Send a Copy to Anyone Else?

Often, people are tempted to send a copy of an email or letter to other people who may or may not be involved. In the above case, the disgruntled client mentioned that his wife and his attorney agreed with him. The mediator considered sending his BIFF to her and to his attorney but realized that doing so would be likely to make the issue grow larger. One principle with high-conflict people is to keep the conflict small. If copied, the wife and the attorney might have asked the client questions about what he wrote; the client probably would have felt defensive, since his request was rejected; and they all may have escalated criticisms of the mediator or of the client.

In this case, the client did not indicate that he had copied his lawyer or his wife, so the mediator did not copy anyone either. However, if a potentially high-conflict client does copy other people, it is often a good idea to copy the same people on your BIFF. Otherwise, it may appear that you didn't respond or someone may believe the complaining person and spread the misinformation around as if it's true. This is especially likely if they copy a lot of people, which high-conflict people often do. Better to clear it up briefly with a BIFF.

Conclusion

This one case demonstrates several issues that come up with potentially high-conflict clients. In mediation, as in all legal services, some clients feel that they did not get their money's worth. In some cases, this may be true, and refunding some or all of a client's money may be appropriate. However, high-conflict clients may want money back that was earned fair and square.

It is always a judgment call when there is an inappropriate

request for a refund. You must weigh the possibility of future hassles against just giving in. Unfortunately, many high-conflict people have learned that making a lot of noise can get them what they want. In the long run, it's better to set realistic limits and get consultation on whether your response is a good one. In this case, the client's request was inappropriate but minor. The mediator declined to respond to the request for a refund, and it worked.

Another judgment call for anyone responding to a hostile communication is whether to copy other people on your response. On the one hand, you want to keep the conflict small and involve as few people as necessary in quietly managing the dispute. On the other hand, if the other party has already copied several people, it may be effective to copy the same people on your BIFF Response. Otherwise, the client's email may get spread around as factual when it is not. Once they have heard from both sides of a conflict, most people prefer to simply stay out of it. If you use a BIFF Response, you may appear to be the more credible and responsible party.

PART 3

Correspondence with Colleagues

CHAPTER 11

Responding to Hostile Opposing Counsel on Minor Issues

It is common nowadays to receive hostile emails and letters from opposing counsel. At continuing legal education programs, it is not unusual for there to be a presentation on nasty emails that have gone around recently. All communities have some lawyers who do this regularly. You probably know who they are in your area of practice. While it is tempting to respond in kind, it really isn't necessary. A good BIFF Response can take care of the situation quickly and simply. This approach keeps you from getting hooked, so you can move on to more important matters.

Cut-Off Phone Service

From: Fred Jones (attorney for wife)
To: Peter Spalding (attorney for husband)
Subject: Phone service cut off

Hey Pete!

Do you know what your client did this weekend???

He cut off my client's cell phone service!! On the weekend, when the office was closed for reinstating service. It's outrageous that you cover up for him and defend him. Unless you do something about this right away, I'm going back to court for an emergency order. You need to do something about this NOW!!!

Fred Jones, Esq.

Response 1

From: Peter Spalding
To: Fred Jones
Subject: RE: Phone service cut off

Hi Fred:

I checked with my client. He said that he sent your client an email two weeks ago stating that he was no longer paying for her cell phone service, effective the 1st of the month, because he has begun paying her $3000 per month support according to the court order. I have attached a copy of his email.

Please check things out before you hysterically jump to conclusions that my client is always doing something wrong. This seems to happen every Monday morning in this case.

Very truly yours,
Pete

BIFF CHECKER: YES OR NO

IS A RESPONSE NECESSARY?	Yes	You should almost always respond to opposing counsel, especially when he or she is upset. Your nonresponse can hurt you in the eyes of others.
BRIEF? (2 to 5 sentences)	Yes	It's just five sentences.
INFORMATIVE? (who, what, when, where, what for)	Yes	It explains what occurred: the "who did what and when," with a supporting email attached.

FRIENDLY?	No	While Pete gives a helpful explanation, he undercuts it with a nasty comment.
FIRM?	No	Fred is likely to respond to this nasty comment, so it doesn't end the hostile communication.
ADVICE?	No	No advice.
ADMONISHMENTS?	Yes	The paragraph about hysterical comments is a very insulting admonishment.
APOLOGIES?	No	No apologies.

IS IT A BIFF? NO

Response 2

From: Peter Spalding
To: Fred Jones
Subject: RE: Phone service cut off

Hi Fred:

I checked with my client about your concern. He said that he sent your client an email two weeks ago stating that he was no longer paying for her cell phone service, effective the 1st of the month, because he has begun paying her $3000 per month support according to the court order. I have attached a copy of his email, which should clear things up.

Very truly yours,

Pete

BIFF CHECKER: YES OR NO

IS A RESPONSE NECESSARY?	Yes	You should almost always respond to opposing counsel, especially when he or she is upset. Your nonresponse can hurt you in the eyes of others.
BRIEF? (2 to 5 sentences)	Yes	It's just one paragraph.
INFORMATIVE? (who, what, when, where, what for)	Yes	This explains what occurred and adds nothing further. It stops where it should.
FRIENDLY?	Yes	It is sufficiently friendly in that it says "I checked with my client about your concern" and "this should clear things up." Not super friendly, but sufficient.
FIRM?	Yes	It ends the discussion on the issue. There are no hooks to get Fred to respond further.
ADVICE?	No	No advice.
ADMONISHMENTS?	No	No admonishments.
APOLOGIES?	No	No apologies.

IS IT A BIFF? YES

Rewrite the Initial Message

Here is another example of how it would be helpful to rewrite the initial correspondence that you received in BIFF format, before responding to it.

Cut-Off Phone Service

From: Fred Jones (attorney for wife)
To: Peter Spalding (attorney for husband)
Subject: Phone service cut off

Hey Pete!

~~Do you know what your client did this weekend???~~
Your client cut off my client's cell phone service this weekend!! ~~On the weekend, when the office was closed for reinstating service. It's outrageous that you cover up for him and defend him. Unless you do something about this right away, I'm going back to court for an emergency order. You need to do something about this NOW!!~~ Please contact me so we can figure this out.

Fred Jones, Esq.

Rewriting the initial communication here provides the essential message and makes it much less emotionally charged.

Childcare Pickup Interference

From: Ike Mann (lawyer #1)
To: Abdul Thomas (lawyer #2)
Subject: Pickup problem

Hello Abdul,

What nonsense did I hear about your client interfering with my client's pickup time?? My client knew that his time was scheduled for 6 pm, and he purposefully ignored this! We discussed the pickup time on several different occasions, and I am confused as to why there is still a misunderstanding. You must have advised your client to violate the rules we discussed. Unless you do something, I am going back to court to update the order. DO SOMETHING NOW.

If this is not resolved, we will have to go to court regarding this matter! We have both been to court several times, and we know how tiresome and lengthy this process can be. So I really do not want to resort to going to court.

Ike Mann, Esq.

Response 1

From: Abdul Thomas (lawyer #2)
To: Ike Mann (lawyer #1)
Subject: RE: Pickup problem

Ike,

I checked with my client, and they did not mess up their pickup time. It must have been your client who forgot the time. My client is very aware of the agreement in place and would not violate this agreement. Plus, there are other matters that my client is upset about too, and I have not brought them up to you like this. You need to check with your client and ensure they know the proper pickup time.

Abdul Thomas, Esq.

BIFF CHECKER: YES OR NO

IS A RESPONSE NECESSARY?	Yes	It's opposing counsel with an active dispute.
BRIEF? (2 to 5 sentences)	No	The attorney rambles and repeats himself.
INFORMATIVE? (who, what, when, where, what for)	No	This email places the blame back on the other side and does not even address the agreement at hand.

FRIENDLY?	No	The attorney does not start with a "hello" or "dear" and does not sign off with any closing pleasantries.
FIRM?	No	The email never comes to a clear point.
ADVICE?	No	No advice.
ADMONISHMENTS?	Yes	The last sentence is an admonishment. It is sarcastic and unfriendly.
APOLOGIES?	No	Rather than give an apology, the attorney starts to blame the client.

IS IT A BIFF? NO

Response 2

From: Abdul Thomas (lawyer #2)
To: Ike Mann (lawyer #1)
Subject: RE: Pickup problem

Hello Ike,

It seems like there was a mix-up here. I will make sure to check the agreement we drafted and remind my client. It would be great if you could do the same with yours, so we do not run into this issue again. I am happy to set up another conference between our clients to clarify anything if you would like.

Kind regards,

Abdul

BIFF CHECKER: YES OR NO

IS A RESPONSE NECESSARY?	Yes	It's opposing counsel with an active dispute.
BRIEF? (2 to 5 sentences)	Yes	This response is brief and to the point.
INFORMATIVE? (who, what, when, where, what for)	Yes	The attorney provides corrective measures and offers a remedy as well.
FRIENDLY?	Yes	The tone is pleasant. It is not overly friendly, but warmth is unnecessary in this case. The attorney appears to be trying to defuse the situation, which works well here.
FIRM?	Yes	The attorney provides immediate action steps and leaves space for the other attorney to address any remaining concerns.
ADVICE?	No	Not in the typical sense. The attorney asks the other attorney to review the agreement but does not advise him to do so.
ADMONISHMENTS?	No	The attorney is trying to defuse the situation; he does not fuel the fire with further admonishments.
APOLOGIES?	No	Rather than give an apology, the attorney acknowledges the mix-up and takes corrective measures.

IS IT A BIFF? YES

Conclusion

It's easy to get emotionally hooked by insulting or confrontational language from opposing counsel. Remember what we observed in chapter 1 about blamespeak: Usually, the other person's nastiness says more about them than it does about you. Remind yourself, "It's not me; it's their personality." Keeping this perspective makes it easier to deal with their comments in a matter-of-fact BIFF Response so you can move on to more important things.

CHAPTER 12

Responding to Hostile Opposing Counsel on Major Issues

Major issues with hostile opposing counsel can be dealt with in the same way as minor issues: with a BIFF communication. However, you may need to take more time in preparing a response and have someone you respect review what you have written. It's amazing how easy it is to offend others and tip the balance of a case in the wrong direction without even realizing it. It doesn't matter if it's small or large; responding respectfully saves time and stress.

The Missed Mediation

From: Jaime Rodriguez (attorney 1)
To: Maria Lider (attorney 2)
Subject: Mediation session

Hello Maria,

Our clients both agreed to attend coparenting mediation. This was a joint decision that they made together. We could obviously proceed with litigation, but both of our clients are hesitant to follow that route. HOWEVER, for mediation to work, your client has to show up! Last week your client rescheduled the session, and this week he did NOT even bother to call. I do not understand how we can continue with this process without full cooperation.

I am happy to share the agreement to mediate that both of our clients signed. It states their obligations to participate fully. You really need to advise your client on the seriousness of this matter.

This is my last time contacting you about this or we will have to TERMINATE THE MEDIATION!

Best,
Jaime

Response 1

From: Maria Lider (attorney 2)
To: Jaime Rodriguez (attorney 1)
Subject: RE: Mediation session

Hello Jaime,

I apologize for the miscommunication. I sent you a message last week. My client is going through a difficult period with his family and had to miss the last two sessions. I would advise you to check your email again because I already explained all of this. In our mediation agreement, we stated that our clients could miss up to two sessions with no penalties. We are still within that limit; therefore, we should proceed with mediation. My client personally apologized to your client for the delay, so I do not understand why we are getting involved. Let's proceed as usual.

Thanks,
Maria

BIFF CHECKER: YES OR NO

IS A RESPONSE NECESSARY?	Yes	Usually, it is important to respond to opposing counsel. In this case, mediation could settle the matter. If it doesn't work—or even happen—then the case will be litigated for sure. A BIFF Response could make the difference.
BRIEF? (2 to 5 sentences)	No	The message is not particularly brief. It includes unnecessary information.
INFORMATIVE? (who, what, when, where, what for)	Yes	It does explain what happened and the different forms of communication that have been occurring. It also states what should happen moving forward. However, this information is mixed in with apologies and admonishments, so some of it gets lost.
FRIENDLY?	Yes	We can see why Maria is frustrated, especially since the situation does not need to involve her or Jaime, but the overall tone is aggressive. There are friendly greetings, but the body of the email does not match this.
FIRM?	No	This message leaves too much room for a defensive response.
ADVICE?	Yes	The attorney specifically says "I advise you," which would come off as very condescending, especially in this context.
ADMONISHMENTS?	Yes	The email is one long admonishment.
APOLOGIES?	Yes	The attorney starts off the email with an apology but also retracts it with the rest of her message.

IS IT A BIFF? NO

Response 2

From: Maria Lider (attorney 2)
To: Jaime Rodriguez (attorney 1)
Subject: RE: Mediation session

Hello Jaime,

Thanks for letting me know your concerns. It sounds like there was just a miscommunication. My client is fully committed to mediation; he had two unfortunate difficulties come up and has apologized to your client. As we discussed in the mediation agreement, our clients can miss two sessions with just cause. Since this is the case, let's continue the process and encourage them to reach an agreement.

Thank you,
Maria

BIFF CHECKER: YES OR NO

IS A RESPONSE NECESSARY?	Yes	Usually, it's important to respond to opposing counsel. A BIFF Response could make the difference.
BRIEF? (2 to 5 sentences)	Yes	Just five sentences.
INFORMATIVE? (who, what, when, where, what for)	Yes	The email explains the situation and creates forward-facing momentum for the clients and the attorneys.
FRIENDLY?	Yes	The attorney is friendly and eases the tension from the first email.
FIRM?	Yes	The email closes further conversation about the matter, encouraging a positive outcome.

ADVICE?	**No**	No advice.
ADMONISHMENTS?	**No**	No admonishments.
APOLOGIES?	**No**	No apologies. Instead of starting the email with an apology, she acknowledges the miscommunication and focuses on the future.

IS IT A BIFF? YES

Conclusion

This example demonstrates how to easily resolve a matter without getting emotionally hooked into making nasty comments yourself. By responding with a BIFF, you can contain the conflict quite quickly. You will continue to have a working relationship with opposing counsel, so it is worth thinking about ways to preserve this relationship through respectful, nonreactive communication.

CHAPTER 13

Initiating Difficult Issues with Opposing Counsel

A s you've seen from several examples in the book, the BIFF format can be helpful for starting a discussion as well as for responding in one that's underway. Keep in mind that you can usually determine what kind of response you will get by how you approach the other person in the first place. A hostile or snide comment is likely to invite a hostile or snide response. A respectful approach to a difficult issue is likely to invite a serious response.

The Out-of-Date Regulation

In this real case, Attorney Kellogg represents a utility company that has been served with a lawsuit regarding the placement of one of its utility line poles. With the lawsuit was a letter from the plaintiff's attorney attacking the utility company as insensitive, corrupt, and reckless. It is based on a regulation which Attorney Kellogg knows has been revised in the past year, rendering the lawsuit moot. He initiates communication with plaintiff's lawyer.

Draft Communication 1

From: Robert Kellogg (defendant's counsel)
To: James Monroe (plaintiff's counsel)
Subject: Utility Regulation 15604.3

Dear Mr. Monroe,

I represent the Utility Company which you are suing for violation of the placement of a utility pole under Utility Regulation 15604. You are a complete idiot! Haven't you looked up the most recent version of this regulation: 15604.3? It changed last year, so that my client's placement of the pole is totally within the standards and regulations. You're not very good at using your legal research database, are you? Using an out-of-date rule book makes you look pretty silly. I advise you to immediately tell your client and withdraw your suit. My client informs me that we will press for attorney's fees and damages if we have to spend another minute on this matter.

Good luck!

R. Kellogg

BIFF CHECKER: YES OR NO

IS A COMMUNICATION NECESSARY?	Yes	A BIFF Response could stop the case right away.
BRIEF? (2 to 5 sentences)	Yes	It's just a paragraph.
INFORMATIVE? (who, what, when, where, what for)	Yes	It explains that the rule changed and what it is now. However, it goes beyond saying what is necessary.
FRIENDLY?	No	It is attacking and disdainful.
FIRM?	Yes	It puts an end to the discussion, but in such a negative manner it may trigger a hostile response.
ADVICE?	Yes	The attorney specifically says "I advise you," which would come off as very condescending.

| ADMONISHMENTS? | Yes | The email is one long admonishment. |
| APOLOGIES? | No | No apologies. |

IS IT A BIFF? NO

Draft Communication 2

From: Robert Kellogg (defendant's counsel)
To: James Monroe (plaintiff's counsel)
Subject: RE: Utility Regulation 15604.3

Dear Mr. Monroe,

I represent the Utility Company which you are suing for violation of the placement of a utility pole under Utility Regulation 15604. You may not be aware that this rule changed last year and has been replaced by Utility Regulation 15604.3. Under the revision, my client's placement of the pole is totally within the standards and regulations. We recognize your client's concerns, but research has shown that there is no danger from these power lines. This change was not well publicized, which may explain why your client wanted to bring this lawsuit. Please dismiss your lawsuit and notify me of this within the next seven days.

Regards,

R. Kellogg

BIFF CHECKER: YES OR NO

| IS A COMMUNICATION NECESSARY? | Yes | A BIFF Response could stop the case right away. |
| BRIEF? (2 to 5 sentences) | Yes | Just one paragraph. |

INFORMATIVE? (who, what, when, where, what for)	Yes	The email explains the rule change and the research behind it.
FRIENDLY?	Yes	The attorney acknowledges the other party's concerns addresses them. He tries to soften the blow for opposing counsel by saying the change wasn't well publicized (without shaming him for failing to do his due diligence before filing the suit.)
FIRM?	Yes	The facts end any further conversation about the matter.
ADVICE?	No	No advice.
ADMONISHMENTS?	No	No admonishments.
APOLOGIES?	No	No apologies.

IS IT A BIFF? YES

Conclusion

As this example shows, it is wise to refrain from rubbing it in when you are totally right and the other is totally wrong. Developing a reputation for such restraint will win you the respect of your peers, and it is good practice for dealing with harder, less clear-cut issues in the future. Notice that Attorney Kellogg does not put a lot of energy into giving his message a friendly tone. This is because the context is more a business-related matter, compared to high-conflict family matters, such as an acrimonious child custody dispute. Yet his correspondence is sufficiently friendly with the one comment about understanding the client's concerns. The goal is to at least be civil and respectful, if not openly friendly.

CHAPTER 14

Communicating with Experts and Other Professionals

A s a lawyer, you will inevitably work with other profession-als in the course of your client's case. Depending on your practice area, they could be social workers, environmental experts, country condition specialists, professors, therapists, or a myriad of other professionals. This type of interaction poses unique challenges because you are all considered experts or specialists in your particular fields. This can lead to complexity in representation and communication.

Matters become even more complicated when the individual you are dealing with is a high-conflict person. This leads to further breakdown of communication, particularly via email or messaging. When a person is discussing matters in which they have expertise, they may become defensive of their work and process. What should be a joint task, often focused on helping a client, becomes an uphill battle. Miscommunication becomes the norm, and the people who suffer are the clients in need of help.

This is where BIFF can be extremely useful. When you're dealing with complex matters, such as your client's mental health, a key legal issue, or an important next step in your client's case, there is a need to find clarity as quickly as possible. BIFF can be the tool to help you get clear and responsive written communication or the means to set up a quick phone call or in-person meeting to illuminate any outstanding issues. The key to an effective BIFF statement in this circumstance is collaboration. With experts, you want to create a team against the problem, not an adversarial relationship. This will yield the best outcome for your client.

Lawyer Versus Therapist

In this family law example, there are two daughters (ages eight and eleven), who have lived primarily with their mother since their parents' separation last year. The court ordered a fifty-fifty parenting schedule, to begin when a recently appointed therapist thought the children were ready to spend equal time with the father. The court had already ordered a lawyer for the children, and she had begun working on the case six months before. The following example is a written conversation between the children's therapist (who was new to the case and new to high-conflict cases involved in family court) and the children's lawyer (who had a lot of experience in high-conflict family cases). They had spoken once on the phone about issues in the case.

From: Nicki Sanders (children's therapist)
To: Esther Johnson (children's lawyer)
Subject: Parenting schedule

Dear Ms. Johnson,
I have just finished my second therapy session with the two girls in this case. They are anxious and adamant that they do not want to spend any more time with their father, who they currently see eight hours per week. They have demanded, and I have agreed, that I will not pressure them to change the parenting plan. I just wanted to let you know. It will be a long time, if ever, before they feel comfortable living with him half of the time. I will work with my clients on managing their emotions during this hard time.

Sincerely,
Nicki Sanders

Response 1

From: Esther Johnson (children's lawyer)
To: Nicki Sanders (children's therapist)
Subject: RE: Parenting schedule

Dear Dr. Sanders,
Thank you for updating me on the therapy, but you are violating the intent of the court order. Your job is to help the girls prepare for the fifty-fifty schedule, not to agree with them to never fulfill it. Since you began this case, I have noticed them becoming *more* resistant to spending time with their father, not *less* resistant. Whether your position of not expecting them to increase their parenting time with their father has encouraged them to become more negative toward him, I'm not sure. I want to advise you that a full psychological evaluation found no difficulties in the father's parenting skills and behavior toward the girls but did find some concerns about the mother's frequent negative comments about the father. It's your job to help them overcome that.

Regards,
Esther Johnson

BIFF CHECKER: YES OR NO

IS A RESPONSE NECESSARY?	Yes	There's a problem, and it needs to be addressed. The question is whether it would be better to speak in person.
BRIEF? (2 to 5 sentences)	Yes	It's just one paragraph with important information, but it could be a little shorter.
INFORMATIVE? (who, what, when, where, what for)	Yes	It provides some important information, but it also engages in a lot of criticism of the therapist's work.

FRIENDLY?	No	The overall tone is too accusatory and defensive to be friendly. Negative emotions take over the tone of the conversation.
FIRM?	No	The criticism invites a defensive response from the therapist.
ADVICE?	Yes	The lawyer advises the therapist on what her job is and how to do it. Even though the lawyer is citing the court order, the tone is not helpful.
ADMONISHMENTS?	Yes	It has an admonishing tone throughout.
APOLOGIES?	No	No apologies.

IS IT A BIFF? NO

Response 2

From: Esther Johnson (children's lawyer)
To: Nicki Sanders (children's therapist)
Subject: RE: Parenting schedule

Dear Dr. Sanders,
Thank you for your information. I believe that there has been a miscommunication here, and I would like to touch base with you about this case. I know that this is a difficult time for the girls, and I want to find ways in which we can work together to get the best outcome for them.

Are you available for a call tomorrow between 1 pm – 5 pm?

Thank you,
Esther Johnson

BIFF CHECKER: YES OR NO

IS A RESPONSE NECESSARY?	Yes	There's a problem, and it needs to be addressed. This issue is important enough that it needs a live conversation instead of more email back-and-forth.
BRIEF? (2 to 5 sentences)	Yes	The response is brief and to the point.
INFORMATIVE? (who, what, when, where, what for)	Yes	She states that there has been a miscommunication and offers to discuss it directly.
FRIENDLY?	Yes	The first sentence acknowledges that there has been a miscommunication without blaming it on anyone. She shows that she wants to work together.
FIRM?	Yes	She says clearly that she would like to touch base with the therapist and requests a phone call.
ADVICE?	No	
ADMONISHMENTS?	No	
APOLOGIES?	No	

IS IT A BIFF? YES

This is a good example of when an email or text message is insufficient. The two parties need to talk directly. It appears to be a complicated case that needs more explanation and collaboration. The more experienced lawyer is in a position to teach the less experienced therapist how these cases often go, but this is very likely to trigger defensiveness for the therapist if not done sensitively. This situation would be best handled in person, or at least in a live conversation over the phone or on a virtual platform.

Expert's Delayed Report

From: Joanna Hu (environmental expert)
To: Iman Has (attorney)
Subject: Final Report and Testimony

Dear Iman,
I have completed the report. I will send it to you a week before I come for testimony prep. Also, I will need to push preparation back one week. Something has come up and your timeline no longer works for me.
Thanks,
Joanna

Response 1

From: Iman Has (attorney)
To: Joanna Hu (environmental expert)
Subject: RE: Final Report and Testimony

Hello Joanna,
Can you please send the report now? We need the whole team to review it before we start preparation. Also, we cannot push preparation back that late. We are on a tight schedule, and you have already agreed to fly to New York on November 30th. We can push it back two days, but that is it! WE ARE EMPLOYING YOU TO COMPLETE THIS REPORT. Let me remind you that you are under obligation!! We both know that reputation is everything in this field, and I promise you that if you do not complete your work on this case, your reputation will be ruined! Please respond ASAP.
Thanks,
Iman

BIFF CHECKER: YES OR NO

IS A RESPONSE NECESSARY?	Yes	The report is needed, so the possibility of a delay must be addressed. This might be better handled by phone.
BRIEF? (2 to 5 sentences)	No	It is eight sentences long with many unnecessary aggressive words.
INFORMATIVE? (who, what, when, where, what for)	Yes	The email is informative in that it states the reason they need the report sooner and the tight deadline under which they are operating. However, it also contains unnecessary information.
FRIENDLY?	No	The tone is not friendly. Everything the attorney is saying is valid, but there is an undertone of frustration accompanied by a direct threat.
FIRM?	No	It does contain the statement "We can push it back two days, but that is it!" However, that is sandwiched between a question ("Can you please send the report now?") and a threat. The aggressiveness is likely to provoke a negative response rather than end the conversation.
ADVICE?	No	No advice.
ADMONISHMENTS?	Yes	The statement about reputation is an admonishment and a threat.
APOLOGIES?	No	No apologies.

IS IT A BIFF? NO

Response 2

From: Iman Has (attorney)
To: Joanna Hu (environmental expert)
Subject: RE: Final Report and Testimony

Hello Joanna,

Thank you for giving me an update. I would like to follow up on two matters: 1) Will you be able to send the report this week? We need the entire team to review it before we start prepping for your testimony, and 2) We are only able to push back the testimony preparation by two days. We are on a tight timeline and would appreciate your cooperation in keeping things on schedule.

Please let me know as soon as possible if both of these matters can work for you.

We appreciate your help and cooperation on this case.

Thanks,
Iman

BIFF CHECKER: YES OR NO

IS A RESPONSE NECESSARY?	Yes	The report is needed, so the possibility of a delay must be addressed. This might be better handled by phone.
BRIEF? (2 to 5 sentences)	Yes	The response is relatively brief while still relaying the urgency of the situation.
INFORMATIVE? (who, what, when, where, what for)	Yes	It clearly lays out the who, what, when, and where of what is needed and what can be done to achieve this goal.
FRIENDLY?	Yes	The attorney is friendly and expresses appreciation to the expert for contributing to the case. She expresses gratitude.
FIRM?	Yes	It directly asks for a response, which is appropriate in this situation. There is a clear solution here. The report needs to be sent over ASAP, and the testimony preparation can only be moved two days later.

ADVICE?	No	No advice.
ADMONISHMENTS?	No	No admonishments. The attorney focuses on problem-solving instead.
APOLOGIES?	No	No apologies.

IS IT A BIFF? YES

This is a good example of the effectiveness of avoiding all threats and angry words, while still explaining the urgency of the situation and making direct requests. If this message gets no response or an unfavorable response, the attorney can make a follow-up phone call. With this positive tone, there is a greater chance the expert will make an effort, rather than responding defensively.

Expert Demanding Information

From: Thomas Coyne (country conditions expert)
To: Marcelo Merced (attorney)
Subject: Send me the information NOW

Hello Marcelo,

I am happy to help you with this asylum case, but it has been two weeks since I received your response. My time is precious, as I am a professor at the University of Buenos Aires and teaching five courses. I am also working on a book and have several other speaking engagements lined up. Either you send me the information tonight, or I am off the case. This is the end of this discussion.

This is the third email I have sent you regarding this case. I decided to work with you because you are highly regarded in your field, as am I, but MY PATIENCE IS RUNNING F***ING THIN NOW.

Thomas

Response 1

From: Marcelo Merced (attorney)
To: Thomas Coyne (country conditions expert)
Subject: RE: Send me the information NOW

Hello Thomas,

I AM SO SORRY FOR THE DELAY. It has been trial after trial, and I am exhausted and burnt out. I know I should have sent you the information earlier, but I think you should learn how to send a nicer email in the future. If this is really a hassle for you, I am happy to find someone else to help with my client's asylum case. You were recommended to me by another immigration attorney, and I was excited about having you on board. Let's see if it happens.

Best,
Marcelo

BIFF CHECKER: YES OR NO

IS A RESPONSE NECESSARY?	Yes	Especially since time is of the essence.
BRIEF? (2 to 5 sentences)	Yes	The attorney kept it to one paragraph but rambled throughout.
INFORMATIVE? (who, what, when, where, what for)	Yes	The response is informative to the point of providing an excess of unnecessary information.
FRIENDLY?	No	The tone switches from friendly to apologetic to defensive. There are pleasant words here and there, but overall, the email is not friendly. All caps usually doesn't help, even in response to all caps.

FIRM?	**No**	The attorney is rambling and does not give a firm response. He wavers in terms of what to do next.
ADVICE?	**Yes**	"I think you should learn how to send a nicer email in the future" is a mix of advice and admonishment.
ADMONISHMENTS?	**Yes**	See above.
APOLOGIES?	**Yes**	The attorney starts the entire email with an apology, then vacillates between apologizing and admonishing.

IS IT A BIFF? NO

Response 2

From: Marcelo Merced (attorney)
To: Thomas Coyne (country conditions expert)
Subject: RE: Send information

Hello Thomas,

Thank you so much for bringing my attention to this matter. I was in back-to-back trials this month, and my attention was not focused on this case as I would have liked. I appreciate your willingness to work on this case, and I am happy to set up a time to meet by phone or Zoom at your earliest convenience. Please let me know a day and time that works for you this week.

Best wishes,
Marcelo

BIFF CHECKER: YES OR NO

IS A RESPONSE NECESSARY?	**Yes**	Time is of the essence in this case.
BRIEF? (2 to 5 sentences)	**Yes**	Brief and to the point.

INFORMATIVE? (who, what, when, where, what for)	Yes	It explains what has been going on and offers concrete, future-facing solutions.
FRIENDLY?	Yes	The tone is friendly. The attorney inserts niceties at the beginning and end. Also, the attorney has softened the title so as not to feed any hostilities.
FIRM?	Yes	The attorney provides concrete reasons for the delay and is both accommodating and firm in terms of future planning.
ADVICE?	No	No advice.
ADMONISHMENTS?	No	The attorney does not admonish the country conditions expert. Instead, he neutralizes the exchange.
APOLOGIES?	No	Instead of saying, "I am sorry," he acknowledges the reasons for the delay. This provides context for the delay without being overly apologetic.

IS IT A BIFF? YES

By offering to set up a phone call rather than "sending the information tonight," the lawyer is running a risk that the expert will drop out of the case. However, the lawyer says he has other options, so it may be a safe risk and may get a positive response. The lawyer can repair the situation further when they talk on the phone or by videoconference.

Rewrite the Initial Message

Here is another example of how it would be helpful to rewrite the initial correspondence that you received in BIFF format, before responding to it.

Expert Demanding Information

From: Thomas Coyne (country conditions expert)
To: Marcelo Merced (attorney)
Subject: Send me the information NOW[JB1]
Hello Marcelo,

I am happy to help you with this asylum case, but it has been two weeks since I received your response. ~~My time is precious, as I am a professor at the University of Buenos Aires and teaching five courses. I am also working on a book and have several other speaking engagements lined up. Either you send me the information tonight, or I am off the case. This is the end of this discussion.~~

This is the third email I have sent you regarding this case. ~~I decided to work with you because you are highly regarded in your field, as am I, but MY PATIENCE IS RUNNING F***ING THIN NOW.~~ Please respond so that we can figure out the best strategy moving forward.

Thomas

Rewriting the initial message here helps to lessen some of the emotional intensity and focuses on problem-solving together. This will likely illicit a more productive response.

Uncommunicative Social Worker

From: Jenna Hernandez (social worker)
To: Samitah Singh (attorney)
Subject: Client Updates

Hello Samitah,
I hope you are doing well. I just received news that Breanne has been placed in a shelter. Will contact you later.
Best,
Jenna

Response 1

From: Samitah Singh (attorney)
To: Jenna Hernandez (social worker)
Subject: RE: Client Updates

Jenna,

I need more information than that!!!!!! Breanne has an upcoming immigration court date, and she needs to be in attendance! I have been trying to reach you for DAYS! It is your responsibility to keep me updated. Please call me now so we can discuss.

Samitah

BIFF CHECKER: YES OR NO

IS A RESPONSE NECESSARY?	Yes	This is a possible crisis, and information is needed.
BRIEF? (2 to 5 sentences)	Yes	The email is brief and does get to the point without being too wordy.
INFORMATIVE? (who, what, when, where, what for)	Yes	Yes, it makes it clear that the attorney needs immediate information so she can properly represent her client and get her to court.
FRIENDLY?	No	The attorney is hostile and takes her frustration out on the social worker. It is likely that they are both being kept in the dark about their client's situation, yet this response would only make the social worker defensive.
FIRM?	No	The email clearly asks for a response, but because it is reprimanding, the reply may not be positive. This message is unlikely to end the hostile conversation.
ADVICE?	No	No advice.

ADMONISHMENTS?	Yes	There are admonishments; the attorney speaks to the social worker in a condescending manner. This is likely out of frustration, but it will not lead to the social worker being responsive and open.
APOLOGIES?	No	No apologies.

IS IT A BIFF? NO

Response 2

From: Samitah Singh (attorney)
To: Jenna Hernandez (social worker)
Subject: RE: Client Updates

Hello Jenna,
Thank you for letting me know this information. Breanne has an upcoming immigration court date, so it is important that I speak to her as soon as possible to prepare.
Do you know the best way to reach her?
I would be happy to jump on a quick call to discuss this matter.
Thank you for your help,

Samitah

BIFF CHECKER: YES OR NO

IS A RESPONSE NECESSARY?	Yes	This is a possible crisis, and information is needed.
BRIEF? (2 to 5 sentences)	Yes	Brief and to the point.
INFORMATIVE? (who, what, when, where, what for)	Yes	The response expresses the urgency of the situation and says what needs to happen next. It does not provide unnecessary information.

FRIENDLY?	Yes	The tone of the email is calm and friendly. The attorney also offers a way to open up communication.
FIRM?	Yes	The response expresses urgency of getting in contact with the client but does not feed hostility.
ADVICE?	No	Although the attorney is likely frustrated, she does not give advice or tell the social worker how to do her job. She simply requests more information and better communication.
ADMONISHMENTS?	No	Instead of admonishing the social worker for her brief and incomplete message, the attorney tries to remedy the situation and create open communication moving forward.
APOLOGIES?	No	No apologies.

IS IT A BIFF? YES

Conclusion

We want to emphasize the unique relationship lawyers and legal professionals have with experts and other professionals. The foundation of this partnership is collaboration and clarity of communication. BIFF is different in this context than it is in other interactions, because oftentimes what is needed for clear and cooperative communication is a quick phone call. BIFF is certainly useful in all written communications with experts and professionals. At the same time, we suggest that you consider BIFF as a way to set up a quick call or in-person meeting, especially when high-conflict people are involved. The key is to keep in mind your mutual goal of working effectively on the case and helping your client.

PART 4

Correspondence with Staff and Between Staff

CHAPTER 15

Responding to Staff Issues and Complaints

Getting and keeping good staff is often difficult in law offices. The pressures can be intense, and it is a field filled with conflict and crises. Since COVID-19, it has become harder to keep staff, so treating them well while also getting urgent work done is of the highest importance. Many law firms are well run, such that lawyers and staff feel respected and valued. BIFF can help maintain good relations internally as well as with those outside of the law office. Once BIFF becomes routine and is used throughout the firm, it makes everyone's job easier and more enjoyable. It will quickly become second nature.

Staff Complaint About Filings

From: Raisa Kain (legal assistant)
To: Jamal Williams (attorney)
Subject: Last-minute filings

Hello Mr. Williams,

I have been helping you with filings for the past six months. Usually, these filings take hours of preparation, which I am willing to help with. However, on three occasions, you gave me all the materials the night before, and I had to stay in the office overnight. I am happy to be part of this team and work on these filings with you, but I also value my personal time outside of the office. I am not paid overtime after midnight. Therefore, I will not be staying in the office later than necessary, and I know that we can have a better system in place.

Can you send me the materials earlier?

Kindly,
Raisa

Response 1

From: Jamal Williams (attorney)
To: Raisa Kain (legal assistant)
Subject: RE: Last-minute filings

Hello Raisa,

This is the nature of our work. Late nights and last-minute filings. I do not appreciate you sending this via email. You should have come and talked to me about the matter. I really don't know what to tell you about the filings. I do things as they come, and I am also stuck in the office late the night before a filing. If you do not think this job is the right fit for you, then we should have a follow-up conversation. Next time you have an issue, come speak to me directly.

Jamal, Esq.

BIFF CHECKER: YES OR NO 93

IS A RESPONSE NECESSARY?	Yes	It's usually best to respond immediately to staff concerns so they don't fester.
BRIEF? (2 to 5 sentences)	No	The email is longer than five sentences and includes unnecessary information.
INFORMATIVE? (who, what, when, where, what for)	No	The attorney reprimands the legal assistant rather than providing information. The assistant is clearly

		looking for a solution, or she would not have sent the email. The assistant also makes a solid ask of receiving the materials earlier, and the attorney does not address this.
FRIENDLY?	No	The attorney is hostile and scolds the assistant.
FIRM?	No	There is too much rambling and unnecessary information for the email to resolve the problem.
ADVICE?	Yes	Indirectly, there is advice about what to do if the assistant feels the job is too challenging.
ADMONISHMENTS?	Yes	The attorney admonishes the assistant and speaks to her in a condescending manner.
APOLOGIES?	No	No apologies.

IS IT A BIFF? NO

Response 2

From: Jamal Williams (attorney)
To: Raisa Kain (legal assistant)
Subject: RE: Last-minute filings

Hello Raisa,

Thank you for bringing this matter to my attention. I understand the taxing nature of this work, which often involves late nights close to a filing date. There is a possibility I can get you the materials earlier, depending on the case. How about we create an open line of communication, and I can keep you up to date on the materials when I receive them so you can start working on the filing earlier in the week.

Let me know how that sounds.

Best,

Jamal

BIFF CHECKER: YES OR NO 94

IS A RESPONSE NECESSARY?	Yes	It's usually best to respond immediately to staff concerns so they don't fester.
BRIEF? (2 to 5 sentences)	Yes	Brief and to the point.
INFORMATIVE? (who, what, when, where, what for)	Yes	The attorney acknowledges Raisa's request to receive the materials earlier and discusses an open communication strategy moving forward.
FRIENDLY?	Yes	The email is friendly and acknowledges Raisa's difficulties without being condescending. The attorney also creates space for her to follow up with him if she has any concerns about their plan moving forward.
FIRM?	Yes	The response may resolve the issue; at least, it does not feed hostility.
ADVICE?	No	No advice. Instead, the attorney lays out a clear plan moving forward.
ADMONISHMENTS?	No	No admonishments.
APOLOGIES?	No	No apologies.

IS IT A BIFF? YES

Conclusion

By treating staff members with respect, lawyers can solve problems and build stronger relationships for the future. Well-run law firms can generally retain good staff for many years, whereas law offices in which lawyers vent their frustration on their staff often are stuck with a revolving door of employees. Thinking in terms of BIFF can help keep things calm and solve problems quickly. BIFF helps to establish a respectful workplace focused on community and thus improve retention.

CHAPTER 16

Initiating Difficult Issues with Staff

As we observed in chapter 5, "Initiating Difficult Issues with a Client," the BIFF approach is useful not only in responding but also when starting a written conversation. Law offices can be such busy places that it seems there is no time for lawyers and staff to be sensitive to each other. This can lead to abrupt communications. In addition, there is a power differential between lawyers and staff. Sometimes lawyers truly don't realize how their communications come across—until someone quits.

It's important to get in the habit of communicating civilly as well as quickly. Practicing the BIFF method can assist with this. Much internal communication is by email, so it's good for lawyers to pause to make sure their emails are reasonable and respectful, and it's good for staff to assess theirs as well. No matter what your role in the organization, you can use the BIFF Checker to improve your communication.

We'd like to offer two additional tips for lawyers as managers:

1. "Public praise. Private criticism." It's easy to forget this, but it goes a long way to helping employees feel safe and valued.

2. "If you are bringing me a problem, please bring me your proposed solution(s). You are closer to the situation, so your solution may be a big help."

You can incorporate both of these ideas into your BIFFs.

Frustrating Filing System

Initial Email 1

From: Sasha Novack (attorney)
To: Aneeta Singh (legal assistant)
Subject: New Case Filing System

Hello Aneeta,

As you already know, we recently implemented a new case filing system. The instructions were clear. You enter the client information as soon as you receive it and then send me a notification through the portal. I can send you a link to the tutorial again. The tutorial really breaks it down in a digestible manner so anyone watching can understand the basics of how to use the portal.

This is the third time this week that I have not been notified that we have a new client. I plan my entire day around doing case intakes in the morning, and when I learn that there is a new case at the end of the day, I am completely thrown off. I really cannot work under these conditions, and it limits my ability to provide comprehensive representation to my clients. I know this is a new system, but it is ridiculous that there have been so many problems. I am unsure what to do moving forward, but I know I need to receive timely notifications regarding new clients.

PLEASE ADDRESS THIS MATTER IMMEDIATELY.

Best,
Sasha, Esq.

BIFF CHECKER: YES OR NO

IS A COMMUNICATION NECESSARY?	Yes	One way or another, this issue interferes with office efficiency and creates frustration—as systems often do. However, a direct conversation might be better than an email.
BRIEF? (2 to 5 sentences)	No	It's long and contains unnecessary venting.
INFORMATIVE? (who, what, when, where, what for)	No	Sasha eventually says what she wants (timely notifications regarding new clients), but the message is mostly venting.
FRIENDLY?	No	It is mostly criticism, with no friendly words. All caps are never called for—especially not with a staff person.
FIRM?	No	Since it is mostly criticism, it is likely to trigger a defensive response, although the legal assistant is in a one-down position and may not complain—for now.
ADVICE?	No	No advice.
ADMONISHMENTS?	Yes	The whole email feels like an admonishment, talking down to the legal assistant and suggesting she doesn't know what she's doing and should.
APOLOGIES?	No	No apologies.

IS IT A BIFF? NO

While this may feel to the lawyer like a routine and neutral communication, and while it isn't directly attacking, it can come across as insulting and demeaning to the staff person (especially due to phrases like "the instructions were clear" and "it is ridiculous"). By going through the BIFF Checker, the lawyer may realize she needs to be more positive and less critical. The two are on the same team, and the lawyer will be better off in the long run if she communicates in a friendly manner. If she doesn't, this employee might become resentful over time from being talked down to this way and quit.

Initial Email 2

From: Sasha Novack (attorney)
To: Aneeta Singh (legal assistant)
Subject: New Case Filing System

Hello Aneeta,

Thanks for dealing with this new case filing system. Unfortunately, it still isn't working well for me. I try to handle my case intakes in the morning, but sometimes I only learn about a new case at the end of the day, which makes it much harder to deal with. Can you please look into this? I really appreciate it.

Best,
Sasha, Esq.

BIFF CHECKER: YES OR NO

IS A COMMUNICATION NECESSARY?	Yes	One way or another, this issue interferes with office efficiency and creates frustration—as systems often do. However, a direct conversation might be better than an email.
BRIEF? (2 to 5 sentences)	Yes	At five sentences, this email is brief and to the point.
INFORMATIVE? (who, what, when, where, what for)	Yes	She explains the problem in one sentence and then makes her request. No arguing or venting.
FRIENDLY?	Yes	The email starts and ends in a respectful and friendly manner ("Thanks" and "I really appreciate it").

		There are no all caps.
FIRM?	Yes	This email is direct and leaves no hooks to trigger the other person.
ADVICE?	No	No advice.
ADMONISHMENTS?	No	No admonishments, just a straightforward request.
APOLOGIES?	No	No apologies, just an explanation of the problem.

IS IT A BIFF? YES

This is the way the lawyers should talk to their staff. It took less time and space to write as a BIFF, and this version showed the legal assistant that the lawyer saw her as a team member to be appreciated.

Now, suppose Aneeta received the first version of the email. How should she respond? Remember that the way an initial communication is written often determines the type of response one gets: positive or negative. What type of response does the lawyer invite? Is this a BIFF Response?

Response 1 (to Initial Email 1)

From: Aneeta Singh (legal assistant)
To: Sasha Novack (attorney)
Subject: RE: New Case Filing System

Hello Sasha,
I told you last week in your office that the new system is not working correctly. This is out of my control. You need to talk to IT, not me.

Thanks,
Aneeta

BIFF CHECKER: YES OR NO

IS A RESPONSE NECESSARY?	Yes	Sasha is Aneeta's boss, and she asks for (demands) a response.
BRIEF? (2 to 5 sentences)	Yes	Very brief and to the point. However, it feels abrupt.
INFORMATIVE? (who, what, when, where, what for)	No	Since Aneeta is the legal assistant, there is likely more that she can find out about the system before responding to Sasha. This reply is an unhelpful nonresponse.
FRIENDLY?	No	The tone is curt and defensive. There is a "thank you" at the end, but following the message, it seems passive-aggressive.
FIRM?	Yes	The message is firm, but it invites an angry response, so it probably won't resolve the issue.
ADVICE?	Yes	Aneeta advises Sasha to talk to IT. This advice could be taken as aggressive.
ADMONISHMENTS?	Yes	Aneeta is indirectly admonishing Sasha for bringing this issue up again via email. She rudely references another conversation they had about the same matter.
APOLOGIES?	No	No apologies.

IS IT A BIFF? NO

Even though the legal assistant is responding to the Initial Email 1, which was quite negative, she herself can shift the conversation by using a BIFF Response. Does the response below accomplish that?

Response 2 (to Initial Email 1)

From: Aneeta Singh (legal assistant)
To: Sasha Novack (attorney) Subject
Subject: RE: New Case Filing System

Dear Ms. Novack,

This is a very frustrating situation, and I will work on getting this resolved. I spoke with IT last week, and they said that you should be getting notifications immediately, but that does not seem to be happening. I will check in with you tomorrow morning to see if the issue is resolved.

Please let me know if there is anything I can do in the meantime.

Thank you,
Aneeta

BIFF CHECKER: YES OR NO

IS A RESPONSE NECESSARY?	Yes	Sasha is Aneeta's boss, and she asks for (demands) a response.
BRIEF? (2 to 5 sentences)	Yes	Brief and to the point.
INFORMATIVE? (who, what, when, where, what for)	Yes	She acknowledges the current situation and provides information about moving forward.
FRIENDLY?	Yes	The email starts and ends in a respectful and friendly manner. The overall tone of the email is neutral but warm.
FIRM?	Yes	There is a solid game plan at the end of the email with space for questions.

ADVICE?	No	No advice.
ADMONISHMENTS?	No	There are no admonishments. Aneeta was likely frustrated by Sasha's earlier email, but she does an excellent job sticking with information and a solution.
APOLOGIES?	No	There is no "sorry." By acknowledging that the situation is frustrating, Aneeta validates Sasha's annoyance, even if it is not Aneeta's fault.

IS IT A BIFF? YES

Conclusion

This exchange is a good example of how lawyers and staff can work together. It also shows the importance of the BIFF Checker questions, especially when writing a quick internal email. There may be no time to run it by another person before sending, so by asking yourself these questions—whether you're the lawyer or the staff person—you can avoid inciting conflict unnecessarily. When a whole law office uses BIFF, it gets easier and easier to keep things positive in the workplace. This can create an office culture shift such that congenial communication becomes second nature to everyone involved.

CHAPTER 17

Staff-to-Staff Communication and Conflicts

O ften, lawyers and managers aren't even aware of how communication is going among their staff. Since legal assistants are typically at the bottom of the pecking order in a law office, it is not uncommon for them to take out their frustration on each other. The BIFF method provides a structure for responding civilly and not making things worse.

Assistant Versus Assistant

From: Simi Ashe (legal assistant 1)
To: Tan France (legal assistant 2)
Subject: Scheduling

Hello Tan,

This is the second email I have sent this week because it is a very urgent matter. I am in the process of scheduling a client meeting for the managing attorney. The hearing is coming up in TWO WEEKS, and our supervisors need to meet with the client to prepare them. Since our supervisors are both attorneys on this case, I need you to confirm her availability.

We need to have a better system of accountability because now I am taking a lot of heat for this entire situation. What do you propose we do moving forward if anything…

Send confirmation ASAP.
Simi

Response 1

From: Tan France (legal assistant 2)
To: Simi Ashe (legal assistant 1)
Subject: RE: Scheduling

Hello Simi,

I just got off the phone with my supervisor, and he said a meeting is unnecessary since the hearing was moved to next month. I would advise you to check for updates before sending out threatening emails. We are both in the same position, and I do not appreciate being talked to like that. I know that you are very on top of scheduling, as am I. In the future, it would be better to call or come to my desk if you are unsure about such matters. Since we will continue to work together, I will excuse your last email.

Best,

Tan

BIFF CHECKER: YES OR NO

IS A RESPONSE NECESSARY?	Yes	Tan and Simi are both responsible for scheduling. Plus, the situation has changed and Simi needs to be informed.
BRIEF? (2 to 5 sentences)	No	The email includes lots of extra verbiage.
INFORMATIVE? (who, what, when, where, what for)	Yes	The email provides some critical information, such as the change in the hearing date. However, it also contains unnecessary admonishments and advice. Since Tan is rambling, the informative part of the email might be lost on the reader.

FRIENDLY?	No	Although there are parts of the email that read friendlier, the overall tone is negative.
FIRM?	No	There is too much rambling for it to be firm. The final question ("What do you propose we do moving forward if anything") makes it unlikely that this message will resolve things.
ADVICE?	Yes	There are two instances in which Tan gives advice. In one, Tan says explicitly, "I advise you."
ADMONISHMENTS?	Yes	There are admonishments for the way Simi handled the situation. Although it is fair for Tan to communicate his frustrations, he did so incorrectly here.
APOLOGIES?	No	No apologies.

IS IT A BIFF? NO

Response 2

From: Tan France (legal assistant 2)
To: Simi Ashe (legal assistant 1)
Subject: RE: Scheduling

Hello Simi,

I just got off the phone with my supervisor, and the hearing has been moved. Since both of our supervisors are working on this case, would it be possible to meet and figure out a way to keep each other up to date on any changes? I am sure we will work together in the future, and I would like to find out the best way to enhance our communication.

Thank you,
Tan

IS A RESPONSE NECESSARY?	Yes	Tan and Simi are both responsible for scheduling. Plus, the situation has changed and Simi needs to be informed.
BRIEF? (2 to 5 sentences)	Yes	Just three sentences.
INFORMATIVE? (who, what, when, where, what for)	Yes	Tan provides information about the current situation and offers future-facing options.
FRIENDLY?	Yes	The email is very friendly and understanding. Tan acknowledges that they will have an ongoing relationship and discusses how to make it better.
FIRM?	Yes	Tan is firm in his response. He leaves room for further conversation but ties up all loose ends.
ADVICE?	No	No advice. Tan simply suggests they work on their communication since they will continue to work together.
ADMONISHMENTS?	No	No admonishments.
APOLOGIES?	No	No apologies. Tan acknowledges Simi's frustration but does not apologize.

IS IT A BIFF? YES

Paralegals in Conflict

From: Joaquin Moses (paralegal 1)
To: Umi Tobias (paralegal 2)
Subject: Affidavit progress

Hello Umi,

What is the update on your affidavit draft that you have been working on with the client? The affidavit should have been submitted to me last week. I was told to review it and send it to my supervising attorney. Since you are new here, you probably don't understand that we submit all case notes on our online filing system. I see that you have not submitted any drafts of the affidavit. It is crucial that we get these drafts in a timely manner. There is a process that we must follow in order to make sure that we are properly serving our clients. We have already discussed this once, and if it is not resolved, I will have to speak with our supervising attorneys.

Send me the finalized draft of the affidavit and upload all of your prior work onto the case management system. If you need more information about how to use the case management system, I recommend that you reach out to Claudia. She is the one who trains us in all of these matters, and it might help to have a refresher course.

Best,

Joaquin

Response 1

From: Umi Tobias (paralegal 2)
To: Joaquin Moses (paralegal 1)
Subject: RE: Affidavit progress

Hello Joaquin,

I have been working directly with your supervising attorney on the affidavit, and he has the final version. I did not know that I need to run everything by you, and I do not appreciate the condescending manner in which you are speaking to me. We are working at the same level, and yes, I am still learning the case management system, but I directly respond to your supervisor. Next time, I am happy to give you an update on any case management questions, but I do not report to you.

Best,
Umi

IS A RESPONSE NECESSARY?	Maybe	A problem has been raised that needs to be addressed one way or another.
BRIEF? (2 to 5 sentences)	No	The message is too long. Umi is repetitive.
INFORMATIVE? (who, what, when, where, what for)	Yes	The message makes clear who Umi is reporting to and gives an update on where the finalized draft of the affidavit is. However, it provides other information that is unnecessary.
FRIENDLY?	No	There are proper opening and closing greetings, but the overall tone of the email is not friendly. It can be read as hostile.
FIRM?	No	There is no firm ending. Umi spends much of the email expressing frustration, which leaves room for a frustrated or retaliatory response.
ADVICE?	No	Although Umi is trying to make clear the hierarchal order and requesting a different way of handling these situations in the future, it's not exactly advice.
ADMONISHMENTS?	Yes	Umi is admonishing the other paralegal for their authoritative stance and their lack of understanding of the hierarchical nature of the office. Since these two paralegals are working together, and likely will continue to do so, admonishing in this way does not create space for a good working relationship in the future.

APOLOGIES?	No	No apologies.

IS IT A BIFF? NO

Response 2

From: Umi Tobias (paralegal 2)
To: Joaquin Moses (paralegal 1)
Subject: RE: Affidavit progress

Hello Joaquin,

I hope all is well.

I believe that there was a miscommunication with your supervising attorney. I have been working directly with him on the affidavit, and he has the finalized version. Since we will be working together in the future, it might be helpful to review the case management system and discuss who we should be reporting to.

Please let me know if you are available to meet this afternoon.

Thank you,

Umi

BIFF CHECKER: YES OR NO

IS A RESPONSE NECESSARY?	Yes	A problem has been raised that needs to be addressed one way or another.
BRIEF? (2 to 5 sentences)	Yes	Brief and to the point.
INFORMATIVE? (who, what, when,	Yes	Umi responds to all the concerns expressed by Joaquin. She also does

where, what for)		not engage in unnecessary discussion, but instead asks for a meeting to clarify.
FRIENDLY?	Yes	The tone is calm and friendly. Umi is likely frustrated, but rather than engaging in the emotional side of the situation, she focuses on joint problem solving.
FIRM?	Yes	Umi suggests a concrete time to meet and discuss the matter rather than leaving the email open ended.
ADVICE?	No	No advice.
ADMONISHMENTS?	No	No admonishments. Umi likely wants to admonish Joaquin for the way he spoke to her, but again does not engage in the emotional aspects of the issue.
APOLOGIES?	No	No apologies.

IS IT A BIFF? YES

Junior Attorney Versus Senior Attorney

From: Selena Johnson (senior attorney)
To: Eric Wu (junior attorney)
Subject: Patent application

Hello Eric,

I am checking in on the patent application that we discussed last week. We need to make it as detailed as possible. There is no room for error in this case. Our client is extremely important and has asked us to complete this application in an expedited manner. I have brought you onto this case because I feel like I can rely on you to complete matters in a TIMELY FASHION. However, it is now overdue and NOT timely. In the future, earlier is better, and I should not have to email you like this for updates!!

Thanks,
Selena

Response 1

From: Eric Wu (junior attorney)
To: Selena Johnson (senior attorney)
Subject: RE: Patent application

Hello Selena,

So, I just completed the patent application. I am honestly pretty upset because after putting it on the hard drive, I saw that there is an identical application you completed last year. It would have really helped to know this information. I wasted three whole days working on an application that you already completed last year.

Here is a copy of the application I drafted. You might just want to use your own application.

Best,
Eric

BIFF CHECKER: YES OR NO

IS A RESPONSE NECESSARY?	Yes	The senior attorney has asked for an update.
BRIEF? (2 to 5 sentences)	Yes	It is brief. However, it also contains unnecessary information.
INFORMATIVE? (who, what, when, where, what for)	Yes	The email is informative. However, it does not provide any forward-facing problem solving. The information is delivered in an aggressive manner.

FRIENDLY?	No	Although it has friendly elements, this email shows too much anger and frustration to be considered friendly overall.
FIRM?	Yes	It is firm, but not in a good way. It essentially cuts off all future conversation, which is not helpful here, since the junior and senior attorney need to continue working together.
ADVICE?	Yes	The junior attorney tells his senior to "use your own application." This may be good advice, but the manner in which he says it is hostile.
ADMONISHMENTS?	Yes	The email is one long admonishment.
APOLOGIES?	No	No apologies.

IS IT A BIFF? NO

Response 2

From: Eric Wu (junior attorney)
To: Selena Johnson (senior attorney)
Subject: RE: Patent application

Hello Selena,

I am attaching the completed patent application. Once I uploaded it to the share drive, I saw that there was an identical application you created last year. I am sure this was an oversight. I suggest that we have a follow-up conversation about the best way to organize the drive so that I have access to your drafts to save time.

Thank you,
Eric

BIFF CHECKER: YES OR NO

IS A RESPONSE NECESSARY?	Yes	The senior attorney has asked for an update.
BRIEF? (2 to 5 sentences)	Yes	It relays what went wrong in a concise manner.
INFORMATIVE? (who, what, when, where, what for)	Yes	It states what the oversight was and suggests ways to prevent the problem from recurring.
FRIENDLY?	Yes	The junior attorney is friendly and gives the senior attorney the benefit of the doubt rather than being accusatory.
FIRM?	Yes	There is a clear solution here: come up with a collective plan on how to organize the drive. This will be accomplished through a follow-up conversation.
ADVICE?	No	No advice.
ADMONISHMENTS?	No	No admonishments. The junior attorney gives the senior attorney the grace that this was an oversight.
APOLOGIES?	No	No apologies.

IS IT A BIFF? YES

Anger on Office Listserv

From: Susan Michelson
To: All Staff
Subject: Updated Policy

Dear Law Associates,

Last week we enacted a new policy in which employees must submit vacation requests four weeks in advance. We understand that several employees have submitted complaints about the policy, and we want to have an open forum where you all can discuss the policy with the managerial team. Below are two options for meeting dates. You may also state any agenda items you wish to discuss. Please email your date preference to Claudia Gomez.

Tuesday, April 11th at 1 pm
Thursday, April 13th at 3 pm

Thank you,
Management

Response 1

To: All Staff
From: Moesha Sinha
Subject: RE: Updated Policy

Dear All,

This new policy is insane. If we are already in conversation with our manager and they approve, why do we need to go through extra hoops?? I have been an employee at this firm for fifteen years, and I have never had to deal with so much bureaucracy. We have earned our vacation, and we should not be penalized for taking it.

Best,
Moesha

BIFF CHECKER: YES OR NO

IS A RESPONSE NECESSARY?	No	There was no need to send this. However, we will continue with the BIFF Checker as if it was necessary. Note that Moesha replied all.
BRIEF? (2 to 5 sentences)	Yes	Just four sentences.

INFORMATIVE? (who, what, when, where, what for)	No	The email did not address what was being asked, which was the recipient's preference in a scheduling matter.
FRIENDLY?	No	The message is angry and hostile, and the sender chose the wrong forum.
FIRM?	No	There is too much rambling and unnecessary information for it to be firm and end the exchange.
ADVICE?	No	No advice.
ADMONISHMENTS?	Yes	The email response is all admonishment. Although the employee's complaints may have merit, this was not the right venue to express these concerns. Management created space for an open dialogue.
APOLOGIES?	No	No apologies.

IS IT A BIFF? NO

Response 2

From: Moesha Sinha
To: Claudia Gomez
Subject: FWD: Updated Policy

Hello Claudia,

I would like to select the option for Thursday, April 13th, at 3 pm. I am also including the following agenda items to discuss at the company-wide meeting:

Systems in place that work
Ways to update existing policies on an individual basis

Best,
Moesha

BIFF CHECKER: YES OR NO

IS A RESPONSE NECESSARY?	Yes	The initial email asked recipients' preference for a meeting date. Notice that Moesha sent this reply to Claudia, as requested, rather than to the entire staff.
BRIEF? (2 to 5 sentences)	Yes	Very brief, focusing on the two questions that were asked in the initial email.
INFORMATIVE? (who, what, when, where, what for)	Yes	The response gives concrete information regarding date and time selection, as well as agenda items.
FRIENDLY?	Yes	The email may not be especially friendly, but it is professional, which is what is called for in this case.
FIRM?	Yes	The response ends the conversation; it does not introduce unnecessary information.
ADVICE?	No	No advice.
ADMONISHMENTS?	No	No admonishments.
APOLOGIES?	No	No apologies.

IS IT A BIFF? YES

Conclusion

This chapter has featured several staff interactions of the kind that can strain working relationships and add to everyone's stress. Internal email communication is important to the smooth running of the law office and keeping it BIFF can make everyone's work easier and more enjoyable. This means refraining from venting and instead staying focused on communicating the essentials in a respectful way. Even in the face of pressures and mistakes, you can choose a tone that conveys that "we're on the same team." In addition, regular positive feedback can be invaluable in maintaining healthy and happy office relationships. Remember to praise publicly and critique privately.

CHAPTER 18

Correspondence with Court Staff

Court staff have a thankless job, dealing with the public all day on intensely personal matters in a confusing system. High-conflict people often find their way into the court system because of their adversarial view of relationship problems, and they frequently vent their frustrations on frontline staff. Yet court staff play a highly important role in the handling of matters from simple to complex. If you treat them well and make their job easier, they will often help you navigate rules (and sometimes technology) to make your job easier. Many times, we have been saved from minor errors and tight deadlines by friendly court staff who we had treated well. Let's take a look at how you can use BIFF in your communications with court staff.

Surprise Hearing Date Change

From: Samantha Stan (court staff)
To: Rishi Kumar (attorney)
Subject: New Hearing Date

Hello Mr. Kumar,

Your client's hearing has been rescheduled. Details to follow.

Samantha

Response 1

From: Rishi Kumar (attorney)
To: Samantha Stan (court staff)
Subject: RE: New Hearing Date

Hello Ms. Stan,

I just received a notification that my client's hearing date was changed...AGAIN. I am unsure what happened this time, but my client is extremely frustrated. I know that COVID-19 has clogged up the court system, but I don't know what to tell my client anymore. We have been preparing for this hearing for TWO YEARS. This time the notification did not even state a specific date for the next hearing.

How do I find out? What do I do in this situation?

Sincerely,
Rishi, Esq.

BIFF CHECKER: YES OR NO

IS A RESPONSE NECESSARY?	No	A response might not be necessary. The email from the court staff said "details to follow."
BRIEF? (2 to 5 sentences)	No	Long-winded.
INFORMATIVE? (who, what, when, where, what for)	No	This email mainly expresses frustration. There is a part at the end asking what to do next, but the attorney is not providing information to the court staff.
FRIENDLY?	No	Although the attorney acknowledges the likely reason for the delay, his annoyance and frustration are evident.

FIRM?	No	The attorney rambles and provides unnecessary information. This email will not resolve anything.
ADVICE?	No	No advice.
ADMONISHMENTS?	Yes	The attorney indirectly admonishes the staff and the court system. His frustration is understandable, but expressing it in this context will not help the situation.
APOLOGIES?	No	No apologies.

IS IT A BIFF? NO

Response 2

From: Rishi Kumar (attorney)
To: Samantha Stan (court staff)
Subject: RE: New Hearing Date

Dear Ms. Stan,

Thank you for the notification that my client's hearing date has changed. This is a little frustrating, since we have been waiting two years, but I know that the court system is clogged right now because of COVID-19.

What do you recommend I do to receive a new court hearing date?

Thank you,

Rishi

BIFF CHECKER: YES OR NO

IS A RESPONSE NECESSARY?	No	Again, a response might not be necessary, since the email from the court staff said "details to follow." But we'll evaluate this assuming Rishi wants to respond.
BRIEF? (2 to 5 sentences)	Yes	Brief and to the point.
INFORMATIVE? (who, what, when, where, what for)	Yes	The main point of this email is to request guidance on what to do next, which the attorney does at the end.
FRIENDLY?	Yes	Although the attorney expresses frustration, his tone is friendly from start to finish, with words like "dear" and "thank you."
FIRM?	Yes	The attorney asks a clear question.
ADVICE?	No	No advice.
ADMONISHMENTS?	No	No admonishments.
APOLOGIES?	No	No apologies.

IS IT A BIFF? YES

Delayed Divorce Judgment Paperwork

Initial Email 1

From: Fred Conway, Esq.
To: Court Clerk
Cc: Family Law Bar Association
Subject: Delayed Divorce Judgment

Dear Clerk:

I submitted a complete divorce judgment for the court clerk's routine approval two months ago. WHERE IS IT!!! I did everything right, and the court clerk has routinely approved other divorce judgments of my colleagues', which were submitted less than two months ago at the suburban courthouse. This downtown courthouse is the worst!! My client is getting remarried in two weeks, so time is of the essence! You must understand the urgency of this! Get this finished immediately, or I'm coming down to court to speak to your supervisor!

Respectfully,
Fred Conway, Esq.

BIFF CHECKER: YES OR NO

IS A COMMUNICATION NECESSARY?	Maybe	This is an urgent matter, but it might be better dealt with in person at the courthouse.
BRIEF? (2 to 5 sentences)	No	This email is longer than necessary.
INFORMATIVE? (who, what, when, where, what for)	Yes	It informs the court that time is of the essence, though it vents emotions and adds a threat.
FRIENDLY?	No	Not at all. It's demanding. Notice also that the lawyer copied the Bar Association. This is likely to insult the clerk and escalate the matter unnecessarily.
FIRM?	No	This doesn't resolve a conflict, it escalates one, possibly involving the Bar Association.
ADVICE?	No	No advice.
ADMONISHMENTS?	Yes	The attorney admonishes the court to get this done or he's coming to talk to the supervisor.

| APOLOGIES? | No | No apologies. |

IS IT A BIFF? NO

Initial Email 2

From: Fred Conway, Esq.
To: Court Clerk
Subject: Delayed Divorce Judgment

Dear Clerk:

I submitted a complete divorce judgment for the court clerk's routine approval two months ago. My client's name is Jane Smith. Can you let me know the status? My client is getting remarried in two weeks, so time is of the essence. Let me know if it would expedite things for me to come down to the courthouse. My phone number is (555) 555-5555.

Thanks so much! I appreciate all the hard work that you do for our families.

Respectfully,
Fred Conway, Esq.

BIFF CHECKER: YES OR NO

IS A COMMUNICATION NECESSARY?	Maybe	This is an urgent matter, but it might be better dealt with in person at the courthouse.
BRIEF? (2 to 5 sentences)	Yes	The message is no longer than necessary.
INFORMATIVE? (who, what, when, where, what for)	Yes	The attorney lets the clerk know when he submitted the judgment, the client's name, and the reason it is an urgent matter.

FRIENDLY?	Yes	He expresses appreciation for the clerk's hard work. (He also doesn't copy the Bar Association.)
FIRM?	Yes	It may resolve the matter, or he is willing to come downtown to court. No hostilities are created.
ADVICE?	No	No advice.
ADMONISHMENTS?	No	No admonishments; appreciation instead.
APOLOGIES?	No	No apologies.

IS IT A BIFF? YES

Conclusion

Most lawyers and law office staff recognize the importance and difficulty of a court clerk's job. It is wise to work with them and not against them. You don't want to get a reputation within the court system for being difficult. You will likely have a continued relationship with court staff, so you'll want to remember the importance of maintaining these relationships. Court clerks and staff have enough stress from working with the public, which often blames the court system for many of their own life problems. No need to add to that stress!

PART 5

Coaching Staff and Clients in Using the BIFF Method

CHAPTER 19

Teaching the Ten Questions

W hether you are teaching the BIFF method to a client, a staff member, a colleague, a family member, or another person, we recommend that you do it using the ten questions in this chapter. These questions can be asked by any person coaching another person who is preparing an email, text, or letter. When you're coaching people in the BIFF method, let them know that they can ask themselves these same questions when they are on their own with no one else around to coach them on what they have written.

Restraint for Lawyers

For years, lawyers have been rewriting their clients' emails, to lower the hostility and to better explain what needs to be communicated. While this approach is sometimes necessary, the problem is that clients don't learn for themselves how to write clearly and calmly. In order to really train someone in using the BIFF communication method, it is essential that you restrain yourself from doing it for the other person. Instead, teach the method by asking these ten questions in exactly this order. This way, your coachee (client, colleague, etc.) can memorize the process. Your coachee can also post these questions near their computer for easy reference. Avoid giving your feedback on the coachee's draft correspondence until Question 10. Restrain yourself! We know it's hard, but it's worth it in the long run.

Ask the first nine questions without getting into a discussion about them. When you ask the client "Is it Brief?" and your clients says "I'm not sure. What do you think?" you must resist the urge to tell them your opinion right away. Instead, say "Hold that thought. We'll come back to it in a few minutes. Now, is it Informative?" And so on, down to Question 9, when you encourage your client to discuss their concerns about what they have written and how they might change it (or not). Only at Question 10 do you give your own input. This way, the coachee learns to think it through. This prepares them to do it on their own when you are not there to help.

The Ten Questions

1. Is it Brief?
2. Is it Informative?
3. Is it Friendly?
4. Is it Firm?
5. Does it contain any Advice?
6. Does it contain any Admonishments?
7. Does it contain any Apologies?
8. How do you think the other person will respond?
9. Now, is there anything you would take out, add, or change?
10. Now, would you like to hear my thoughts about it?

Explaining the Method

Here's how you can explain each of these questions to your client, staff member, or other coachee:

Is it Brief?

Make it just one paragraph, if possible. Four to six sentences are usually sufficient, no matter the length of the correspondence to which you are responding. This isn't a brief to be filed at court. That said, one sentence may be too brief. If you are *initiating* a correspondence (rather than responding), your message may need to be a little longer; for instance, it may take two paragraphs to explain what the issue is and make your request. Still, try to keep it relatively brief.

Is it Informative?

Focus on logistical information, such as the Who, What, When, and Where of an event or issue. Keep it to straight information, without defenses, arguments, opinions, emotions, or judgments. While it's tempting to add these things, they actually weaken your message by distracting the person and triggering emotional responses unnecessarily.

Is it Friendly?

Try to include a few friendly words to avoid escalating hostility. For example, you might say "Thank you for letting me know your concerns" or "Thank you for responding." Near the end, you might include something like: "I appreciate your hard work on behalf of this organization" or "Have a good weekend" or "Safe travels!" It doesn't have to be overly friendly; you're just trying to set a positive tone. In some situations, it will be acceptable or even preferable to be merely professional rather than friendly. At the very least, be civil in your correspondence.

Is it Firm?

The question of firmness can be confusing. Your goal is to try to completely end the hostilities or confusion, without adding anything to hook the other person into continuing an unnecessary conflict. Avoid saying "What do you think of that, Buddy?" That just feeds the conflict, when you want to resolve it, or at least put an end to a hostile discussion. Firm does not mean harsh! Avoid confronting the other person or telling them how it is or what to do. Save your energy and focus on information that may solve a problem or make the dispute not worth pursuing.

Does it contain any Advice?

An angry or misinformed person is not looking for advice from their target of blame. Advice will usually just trigger a new argument disagreeing with the advice. It is especially tempting for attorneys to put on their lawyer hat and dispense advice to anyone, including those who are criticizing them. This is not the place to do that! Just forget about it. Parents and adult children especially like to give each other advice, after growing up with it as a one-way street.

Does it contain any Admonishments?

Admonishments go further than advice, insulting the other person by treating them as ignorant or stupid. (It is not unusual for high-conflict lawyers to communicate this way with other lawyers, saying things like "You wouldn't understand" or "If you were a *real* lawyer...." Don't take the bait!) When people are misinformed, it is very tempting to admonish them for being uninformed by telling them what they *should* do. Anything that could be interpreted as a "should" is to be avoided in a BIFF communication, because it is likely to trigger a defensive response. No one likes to be insulted.

Does it contain any Apologies?

The guidance to avoid apologizing is the biggest surprise to many people. Gently explain that apologies are a very good thing with ordinary people, but high-conflict people (or people who are just really angry) often misinterpret apologies for little things as admissions of guilt for everything in the relationship. ("See here, he admits that he was wrong, that it was All His Fault!") Because of the all-or-nothing thinking that is characteristic of high-conflict people, the smallest apology can be twisted around into something huge. Since they cannot accept any responsibility for problems in relationships, they are looking for things that help them point the other way. Just steer clear of this. No blame either way.

Instead, you can explain how a problem occurred and how you are going to make sure it doesn't happen again. We can control the future, not the past, so this is where the focus should be, rather than on apologizing for the past. If you still feel that you must apologize, it's better to do it in person so you don't have a paper trail that can be used against you. Avoiding apology is especially important for survivors of domestic violence and women in the workplace. In these cases, apologizing is often automatic, but it may weaken your power in the relationship or organization. We often refer to this as Apology Quicksand.

How do you think the other person will respond?

Encourage the coachee to read what they have written out loud while picturing the other person hearing it. This is an important and often forgotten step. By imagining the other person's reaction, the writer may realize that certain words or phrases are likely to be triggers for the other person that will escalate the conflict unnecessarily. It is common to take out or rewrite phrases or whole sentences after picturing how the first draft will sound to the other person.

Now, is there anything you would take out, add, or change?

This is the point where you can encourage the coachee to tell you his or her thoughts about what they wrote and problems they have detected. Encourage the coachee to try reading it out loud with their proposed edits. If the coachee asks you what you think about a potentially concerning phrase or sentence, try not to share your thoughts yet; save them for Question 10. Instead, have the coachee read the whole draft out loud with the questionable part and then read it out loud again without the questionable part. This usually makes the best course clear to the writer, and they make their own decision about whether to include it. More often they realize it's better without the suspect phrase or sentence—briefer is usually best. This exercise also helps them in the future when they are writing on their own.

Now, would you like to hear my thoughts about it?

After a full discussion of the coachee's own thoughts about their draft, go to Question 10: Do you want to know my thoughts about it? Usually, they say yes. If the person says no, then you're done. But if they say yes, then you can give your input—any input. Don't overwhelm them with too much feedback, or they may become discouraged. Sometimes, just one or two suggestions are plenty.

After your input, tell them "These are just my thoughts. It's up to you! It's your writing. You will be the sender." This is the truth, and by expressing it to your coachee, you are less likely to be blamed if the message still gets a negative response despite both of your efforts. Remind your coachee that while they can try to influence the conversation in a positive direction, they cannot control how the other person will respond.

Conclusion

Teaching the BIFF communication method is relatively easy, and most people who learn the method teach at least one other person. However, it's important to teach the Ten Questions in exactly this fashion, so that the coachee learns to write BIFFs properly on their own. Resist the urge to step in and tell them how they should have done it from the start. Help your coachee learn by breaking it down into these little steps. By using this step-by-step approach with lots of encouragement and practice, even high-conflict people have learned the BIFF method.

CHAPTER 20

It's Up to You!

As we said from the start, you can largely determine how others will respond to you, especially in your writing. If you use blamespeak, you will tend to get more blame in return. If you use BIFF communications, you are more likely to get a positive or at least neutral response. It's up to you!

We have given you dozens of examples of how *not to* respond to hostility or misinformation, and how *to* respond using the BIFF format. We have also explained how you can initiate a correspondence using the same BIFF method by keeping it *Brief, Informative, Friendly,* and *Firm*.

Using this method with law clients can simplify your communication and reduce conflicts. Teaching this to your law office staff can help create a culture of positivity even while you all handle lots of difficult legal and personality problems every day. Law practice can be stressful, and lawyers have a relatively high rate of stress and dislike for their jobs. BIFF can help make it possible to work together better, support each other, and enjoy helping your clients improve their own lives regardless of what others say or do.

If you teach your clients or staff the BIFF method, keep in mind the Ten Questions. Learning the concept of the BIFF method is relatively easy. But doing it effectively takes practice! A lawyer or staff member should write a number of successful BIFF communications before teaching it to clients or others. It's actually harder than it looks.

No matter how experienced you are, it can still help to get someone else to look over your drafts and give feedback.

We have found that to be true for ourselves, and we still ask for another set of eyes to look at what we have written, especially with highly sensitive subjects and situations. The reality is that in high-conflict situations, our instinctive responses of fight, flight, or freeze often backfire. Instead, we have to regularly override our instincts and craft a measured response. BIFF communications can make the difference.

And since we're all about keeping things brief, we're going to stop here.

Best wishes in keeping your correspondence *Brief, Informative, Friendly,* and *Firm!*

Resources for Learning
the BIFF Method

With High Conflict Institute, we have developed several resources for learning the BIFF approach that can be especially helpful for lawyers, law offices, and their clients.

New Ways for Families:
Online Classes, Coaching, and Counseling

Each of these formats teaches potentially high-conflict parents strategies for managing their coparenting relationship during and after a separation or divorce. The BIFF method is included among many other skills. This training can help family law clients calm their own conflicts and also reduce lawyer time spent on email communication (and avoid the lawyer having to defend their client's awful emails in court).

BIFF for CoParent Communication (2020)

This is a book specifically designed for calming communication between parents in separation and divorce. It includes twenty-eight examples of BIFF communication in response to hostile or misinformed emails, letters, or texts. It demonstrates the use of the BIFF Checker for each of these examples, first with a non-BIFF response and then with a BIFF Response. Parents find this to be a very easy way to learn the BIFF method. Lawyers, therapists, and even judges have recommended this method and this book.

New Ways for Work: Coaching

This is a method we teach workplace professionals for coaching employees or managers who want to improve their conflict-resolution skills or have been told to get coaching for their workplace behavior. In three to eight sessions, a coach (therapist, Employee Assistance Professional, or other trained professional) can teach several skills for reducing and resolving conflicts, including the BIFF method. For lawyers with clients in trouble at the workplace, taking this coaching and learning the BIFF method may make the difference in whether they keep or lose their job. Before an employer decides whether to transfer or terminate someone from their employment, we always encourage coaching to see if the employee can learn to communicate more effectively. Some can and some can't. Coaching gives them a chance to change before such decisions are made.

BIFF at Work (2021)

This book provides thirty examples of potentially high-conflict communications in the workplace and how to write a BIFF communication instead. The book applies the BIFF Checker to each of these examples, first with a non-BIFF communication, then showing a BIFF communication. This book can help lawyers who share it with their management clients, so they can be more effective in replying to high-conflict correspondence. It can help lawyers' employee clients, by teaching them the method and improving their workplace communications.

BIFF: Quick Responses to High-Conflict People, Their Personal Attacks, Hostile Email and Social Media Meltdowns, Second Edition (2014)

This is the original BIFF book, which addresses a wide range of situations, including neighbor disputes, business disputes, and many others. It explains high-conflict personalities and provides numerous general tips to improve anyone's communication.

BIFF Response for Lawyers: Using and Teaching Respectful Communication

This one-hour online video training helps individual lawyers and whole law offices quickly learn the BIFF communication method.

Consultation and Individual BIFF Coaching

We offer consultations with lawyers, law firms, and staff in dealing with high-conflict cases and other professional situations. This often includes applying the BIFF method to a touchy problem. In some cases, law office clients contact us specifically for coaching in the BIFF method.

High Conflict Institute Training

We regularly provide training to lawyers and others at conferences and also to law firms that want personalized training in understanding and managing high-conflict people, and in team building. The BIFF method is one of several essential skills included in each training.

BIFF Certification Training

We provide training and BIFF Certification™ to law firms or any organization that wants to implement BIFF as a communication protocol internally with employees and colleagues, and externally with clients and other professionals. The result is a calmer workplace, significant time savings, and reduced stress.

[First published by California State Bar, *Family Law News*, Issue 2, 2013, Volume 35, No. 2, pp. 25–29. Reprinted with permission.]

Misunderstanding Incivility and How to Stop It

Recently there has been growing discussion of incivility in all areas of modern life. Public figures, professionals, and the public are growing more concerned about this behavior. While this problem appears in every occupation, I am writing this article about the legal profession as a lawyer.

Nowadays, parties in disputes are abandoning lawyers and attempting to represent themselves more than ever before. Students are applying to law schools in fewer numbers than in decades. Worldwide, the view is growing that lawyers are a source of hostility, rather than a profession that manages it. While my points in this article may apply to any occupation today, because the problem is people, the practice of law appears to attract and tolerate more of such people.

As a practicing attorney for fifteen years in Family Courts, I routinely experienced incidents of incivility, especially when I was starting out. As a family mediator—before, during, and after my court practice—I have experienced a few such incidents, but much less so. More recently, as a speaker at bar conferences and judicial trainings on managing "high-conflict" behavior, I am increasingly asked about methods for dealing with rude, obnoxious, and shameful behavior by "high-conflict" counsel.

I am told by judges and lawyers alike that new attorneys are more engaged in this type of behavior. If this is really true, it's hard to tell whether it is a result of new lawyers learning from the worst role models, or from seeing uncivil behavior rewarded instead of stopped, or simply entering the profession as ruder people. Perhaps all of the above.

What I do know is that this problem is not being very effectively addressed and I believe it is because most people misunderstand its dynamics. This article addresses what may be happening and provides a few suggestions for dealing with it.

Persuasion Doesn't Work

On January 28, 2013, a *Wall Street Journal* article reported that some leading New York lawyers joined together to address the problem of incivility in a new way. They rewrote popular songs and performed them at a bar meeting about "lawyers behaving badly." Apparently, it was great fun and succeeded at bringing attention to the problem, but I doubt it had any impact. For years, judges and leading attorneys have given speeches in an effort to inspire their colleagues to "behave." I have attended sincere lectures on civility by justices of the highest courts in several states and provinces, and I have great respect for them. But this hasn't stemmed the increase in this behavior.

For example, in 2007, the State Bar of California adopted the *California Attorney Guidelines of Civility and Professionalism*. The introduction to the guidelines state in part:

"As officers of the court with responsibilities to the administration of justice, attorneys have an obligation to be professional with clients, other parties and counsel, the courts and the public. This obligation includes civility, professional integrity, personal dignity, candor, diligence, respect, courtesy, and cooperation, all of which are essential to the fair administration of justice and conflict resolution."

This is a great set of guidelines for civil behavior, and I was encouraged by this effort. But they have failed to reduce the problem, which has only increased since then. In setting forth these guidelines, the President of the Bar stated:

"As we all know, uncivil or unprofessional conduct not only disserves the individuals involved, it demeans the profession as a whole and our system of justice. A growth in uncivil conduct in the legal profession caused me to initiate the effort for Board adoption of civility and professionalism guidelines.

I hope you will join me in encouraging California attorneys to engage in best practices of civility by making the *Guidelines* their personal standards and goals."[9]

It turns out that "encouraging" attorneys hasn't worked. 80 to 90 percent of lawyers already act civilly with each other and the court. They don't need detailed guidelines about how to behave, because they already routinely act in a civil manner. The 10 to 20 percent who act uncivilly haven't changed. Lack of encouragement isn't the issue for them. They need real consequences if they are going to stop their behavior, and retraining or expulsion from the profession.

Unfortunately, the guidelines avoided enforcement consequences, such as sanctions, specifically saying "sanctions can be expected to lead to a less collegial relationship among counsel, and tend to undermine the civility effort."[10] The hope was that improving the profession would be sufficient reward in and of itself, by improving enjoyment of one's professional work and raising the overall view of lawyers in society. That hopeful approach has failed. So what other approaches are there?

Public Shaming Doesn't Work

In February 2013, on the San Diego Family Law Listserv, one lawyer named another lawyer (I'll just say "Lawyer A") and de-

---

9   Sheldon H. Sloan, Letter to Bar Leaders, July 17, 2009.
10 *Guidelines* FAQs, July 2009.

scribed Lawyer A's uncivil behavior in detail which he ("Lawyer B") thought was outrageous. The uncivil behavior had to do with Lawyer A having a couple of dogs dropped off at Lawyer B's office, without warning or agreement, that were the subject of a divorce dispute and prior unproductive conversations between the lawyers. Apparently, the dogs created quite a management and cleanup problem.

This triggered two Listserv discussions: (1) Was Lawyer A's behavior outrageous? Most of those who responded agreed it was, and some suggested legal actions that could be taken by Lawyer B against Lawyer A. (2) Was it inappropriate for Lawyer B to publicly give Lawyer A's name—was this perhaps uncivil too? This drew heated responses on both sides. The theory of those who supported the public "outing" was that public shaming will lead to better behavior. The other viewpoint was that public shaming is not part of the solution, but part of the problem of incivility. It showed highly negative personal attacks designed to harm another professional's reputation. In a sense, fighting fire with fire. It doesn't make things better and appears to make things worse.

Yet public shaming is an increasingly common approach in our society, even among public figures and even endorsed by some business leaders. For example, Robert Sutton, a management professor at Stanford University, published a popular book in 2007 titled *The No A**hole Rule: Building a Civilized Workplace and Surviving One That Isn't.* In it he argues for the near elimination of a**holes from the workplace, including employees and managers who qualify. (I'm restraining myself here—Sutton spells out the a-word and admits that he "shamelessly" used the word to get attention, which he successfully did.) I agree with many of his concerns and many of his ideas, although I prefer the term "high-conflict people" or HCPs for short, without publicly labeling any individual. But I disagree with his support of public shaming.

For example, he describes a restaurant scene in which someone is bothering a waitress:
One day, I waited behind an especially rude customer who was sitting at the counter. He made crude comments, tried to grab the waitress, complained about how his veal parmigiana tasted, and insulted customers who told him to pipe down. This creep kept spewing his venom until a fellow customer approached him and asked (in a loud voice), "You are an amazing person. I've been looking everywhere for a person like you. I love how you act. Can you give me your name?" He looked flustered for a moment, but then seemed flattered, offered thanks for the compliment, and provided his name.

Without missing a beat, his questioner wrote it down and said, "Thanks. I appreciate it. You see, I am writing a book on a**holes... and you are absolutely perfect for chapter 13." The entire place roared, and the a**hole looked humiliated, shut his trap, and soon slithered out—and the waitress beamed with delight.[11]

A Bar of Soap

The problem with this approach is that it promotes calling people names in public, which is itself seen as uncivil behavior by many people. When I was a teenager, my mother washed my mouth out with soap for using words like that—even in our house!

When restaurant customers or beleaguered lawyers resort to self-help by publicly humiliating someone by name who has been offensive, it looks a lot like there are two a**holes, and the problem often escalates. Sutton admits this about himself in an example in his epilogue, after he first published the book. He was at a concert where he told two noisy, drunken women behind him to quiet down, and they called him an a**hole. So he

---

11 Sutton, Robert. 2007. *The No Asshole Rule: Building a Civilized Workplace and Surviving One That Isn't.* New York: Warner Business Books, pp. 179–80.

said they were the "real a**holes," to which they screamed back "You are the f***ing a**hole, not us!" To his credit, he admits that he may have contributed to the problem in that case.[12]

Identification as a Victim

What many people don't realize is that much or most incivility is justified in the uncivil person's mind by the actions of others. "I had to say what I did after what they said or did to me!" is what I often hear or see in uncivil situations. From my experience with HCPs, efforts to angrily confront them with their own behavior just trigger more defensive behavior, not less. They lack self-awareness of their impact on others and are absorbed in their own arrogance or distress. It appears that their uncivil behavior is part of their personality, rather than an aberration. Negative feedback—especially reciprocal insults—doesn't change their normal approach to life at all. In fact, it reinforces it.

In a book on the development of personality disorders, beginning in childhood or adolescence, the researcher Efrain Bleiberg with the Menninger Institute describes a common pattern he has identified[13], which I have summarized as follows:

When people develop personality disorders, they don't reflect on their own behavior in social interactions, with the following result:

Their behavior becomes rigidly patterned (doing the same thing over and over again).

This causes significant social impairment (they don't have friends and social respect).

Which causes significant internal distress (because people need friends and respect).

---

12 *Id.* p. 202.
13 Bleiberg, Efrain. 2004. *Treating Personality Disorders in Children and Adolescents: A Relational Approach.* New York: Guilford Press.

This rigid behavior "evokes" responses in others which "validate" or justify their inflexible beliefs and behavior in their eyes. ("See, I showed them," they often say, proud of their bad behavior.)

In other words, a person with a personality disorder tends to trigger negative responses in others, but then they don't gain any insight from these negative responses, regardless of how well intentioned the responders might have been. If you think of giving personality-disordered people or "high-conflict" people insight into their own behavior, just tell yourself: "Fuhgeddaboudit!"

Consequences, not insight, are what is needed with such people. But could uncivil attorneys have personality disorders?

Attorneys with Personality Disorders?

When people have a personality disorder, they have a more narrow range of behavior, as described by the mental health handbook, the DSM-IV and the new DSM-5. If incivility is part of that personality-based behavior, then it is an embedded pattern that is generally harder to change than stopping drinking or drug use is for an alcoholic or addict. It's an automatic behavior that the person accepts as "necessary and normal" since those with personality disorders lack self-awareness and behavior change.

According to various studies in the United States, approximately 10 to 20 percent of the general population has a personality disorder.[14,15] They are present across all economic levels,

---

14 Grant, B. F., D. S. Hasin, F. S. Stinson, et al. 2004. "Prevalence, correlates, and disability of personality disorders in the United States: Results from the national epidemiologic survey on alcohol and related conditions." *Journal of Clinical Psychiatry* 65(7), 948–58. https://doi.org/10.4088/jcp.v65n0711

15 Grant, B. F., S. P. Chou, R. B. Goldstein, et al. 2008. "Prevalence, correlates, disability, and comorbidity of DSM-IV borderline personality disorder: Results from the Wave 2 National Epidemiologic Survey on Alcohol and Related Conditions." *Journal of Clinical Psychiatry* 69(4), 533–45. https://doi.org/10.4088/jcp.v69n0404

racial and ethnic groups, age groups, and geographic regions of the country (although slightly higher in urban areas than rural). (Grant, et al. *Journal of Clinical Psychiatry,* July 2004 and April 2008 issues.) To have a personality disorder, one must have significant social impairment and/or internal distress. No one has studied, to my knowledge, whether lawyers as a group have less than the general population, about the same or more. But many people inside and outside the profession believe there is a higher incidence in the legal field—that it attracts high-conflict people, many of whom have personality disorders.

From my experience and observations, this personality-based behavior follows three general patterns in the legal field, whether full personality disorders or just some traits of these disorders:

Narcissists: These attorneys see themselves as superior and allowed to treat others as lesser beings. The common expression is that they see themselves as "a legend in their own mind." They enjoy being uncivil to opposing parties, opposing counsel, and their own clients. Yet they see themselves as outstanding advocates—zealous advocates—for their clients, and they justify every insult they deliver as part of that advocacy role. They think the rules don't really apply to them, and they laugh it off when those "beneath them" (in their eyes) are upset by their behavior. Yet they effectively impress those above them enough, such as judges and leaders in the legal community, that they rarely get confronted with real consequences for their behavior.

Borderlines: Such lawyers can't control their emotions; they are all over the place. They may slam down the phone or blurt out that someone is an a**hole in a negotiation session. They write fiery emails and send them, blasting the other party for being a jerk, totally oblivious to the inappropriateness of what they themselves have written. They always feel on the defensive and go from crisis to (mostly self-created) crisis, dealing angrily with their own clients, staff, and opposing counsel in much the same manner. Yet they are totally surprised when others point out to them that they are acting inappropriately. Some of them even get in trouble for treating the court disrespectfully, because they have difficulty controlling their emotions and their mouths with anyone—even in court.

Antisocials: These lawyers enjoy other people's pain. They freely criticize and manipulate their clients, the opposing parties, and opposing counsel. They ask opposing counsel for favors but rarely return them. The legal profession gives them cover for the behavior they came in with, because they are usually clever enough to cultivate the appearance of being chummy with those in authority positions. This personality in particular is developed by adolescence and very hard to change. Sole practice and family law are areas where they can thrive and engage in misbehavior with little likelihood of consequences. They have a much harder time in large firms where people catch on to them and won't tolerate their daily behavior. But some slip through anyway. They cleverly manipulate the court (such as lying about case precedents or their own actions in a case) and rarely get caught.

All of these personalities are extremely hard to change, and many people have more than one. However, people with just traits of a personality disorder, but not the full disorder, may be more able to change with sufficient consequences and training. All of them identify themselves as victims defending themselves from others, which helps them justify any behavior they engage in. A lecture from the bench or guidelines "encouraging" better behavior will have no impact on them whatsoever. Incivility is part of who they are. It is a defense mechanism fundamental to their personalities. You might as well tell them not to breathe. Instead, there are better approaches.

Of course, it's very important to recognize that personality disorders can be in the eye of the beholder and that even mental health professionals disagree on who fits this diagnosis. Many people with personality disorders don't see it in themselves, but see it in others who are acting reasonably. In fact, that's what drives a lot of litigation when a person with a personality disorder is involved. Which person is it? The focus needs to be on behavior rather than labeling. But uncivil behavior does need to be changed.

Consequences

Based on years of working in mental health settings, family law practice, and studying the research on personality problems, it has become clear to me that changing personality-based behavior requires consequences, much in the same way that treatment for alcoholism and addiction doesn't really begin until there are sufficient and immediate motivating consequences, such as losing a driver's license, a job, or a marriage. I would make the following three suggestions.

Requiring civility as a mandatory CLE topic Itself. For years, there has been a required effort in the legal profession to educate lawyers about alcoholism and addiction, including mandatory continuing legal education (CLE) every two years on the subject and referral services for those in need of a recovery program. I would suggest requiring civility as a mandatory CLE topic for all lawyers itself, not just part of ethics, including descriptions of specific behaviors that are considered uncivil and exposing examples, without naming names, except where there are public cases, such as some recent appellate cases in which lawyers received sanctions.

Lawyers could submit confidential case examples of recent uncivil behavior prior to a CLE seminar, for larger discussion. For example: Is it uncivil to write a letter that states that opposing counsel is "a disgrace to the profession?" Or to throw papers that fall on the ground at opposing counsel just before court is in session? Or to tell a new lawyer "You're not a real attorney" during settlement negotiations? Or to refuse to shake opposing counsel's hand when he or she arrives with a client for a deposition? Or to serve papers on the opposing party at work by two armed marshals when that party's counsel said he would accept service?

Some local bar leaders have begun to take this approach of giving public examples (without names) for discussion, although it's not at a mandatory CLE. Such a CLE should become mandatory until the problem of incivility is significantly reduced, at which time it could become voluntary.

Providing real consequences. Financial sanctions from the court, suspensions of licenses, and disbarment are real sanctions. We are starting to see more court decisions at the appellate level endorsing sanctions against attorneys who have been particularly egregious in their behavior. This is a good thing. Disciplinary action by the bar needs to become more assertive in the civility area. The *Civility Guidelines* are a great idea, but they need enforcement measures. State Bar presidents and committees should build on these efforts.

If the first two suggestions don't produce enough behavior change: Perhaps there should be an effort to requiring civility training for certain attorneys, just as certain lawyers are required to take professional responsibility courses as a disciplinary consequence. After all, recovery from alcohol and drugs takes repeated learning and practice of healthier behaviors, not just a lecture. But first, let's see if the first two suggestions make a difference.

And perhaps it wouldn't hurt if some judges put a bar of soap next to the gavel in their courtroom, as a subtle reminder to lawyers and the parties that we need to act civilly with each other and the public, and that there may be consequences if we don't!

APPENDIX B

Sample Situations and BIFF Responses

RESOURCES

High Conflict Institute
www.HighConflictInstitute.com
Training, consultation and programs for dealing with high conflict personalities and high conflict disputes.

High Conflict Legal Dispute Resolvers Certification™
https://www.highconflictinstitute.com/legal-certification
An online certification course (10 CLE credits) taught by Bill Eddy, LCSW, Esq., for any legal professional to learn advanced skills for managing high conflict legal disputes. The training describes the surprising and predictable patterns of behavior of five high conflict personality disorders, with effective methods for ethically managing them in legal disputes, both in and out of court. Several skills are provided for managing legal clients, opposing parties, and the negative advocates they often persuade to join them in their disputes.

Family Law Consultation Group
https://www.highconflictinstitute.com/bookstores/consultation-group
A monthly 90-minute session with other lawyers and Bill Eddy, LCSW, Esq. to help family lawyers discuss issues that arise in high conflict cases.

On Demand CLE Courses
https://www.highconflictinstitute.com/virtual-courses
Many courses taught by Bill Eddy, LCSW, Esq., for legal professionals that are applicable to all law types.

Books available at https://www.highconflictinstitute.com/store or anywhere books are sold.

High Conflict People in Legal Disputes
By Bill Eddy, LCSW, Esq.

Managing High Conflict People in Court
By Bill Eddy, LCSW, Esq.

Mediating High Conflict Disputes
By Bill Eddy, LCSW, Esq. and Michael Lomax, JD

The Future of Family Court
By Bill Eddy, LCSW, Esq.

ACKNOWLEDGEMENTS

We could not write a book like this without the help of the team at the High Conflict Institute and the guidance provided by Megan Hunter, our CEO. We also want to give our appreciation for the many lawyers, mediators, judges, therapists, and students over the years who attended our High Conflict Institute presentations and gave us feedback when we taught the BIFF method and other skills.

Bill – I also want to acknowledge my mentor attorney when I started practicing law, Bill Benjamin, and my associate attorney during my early years, Tia Wallach. I also appreciate the National Conflict Resolution Center, especially Steve Dinkin, Ashley Virtue, and Kathy Purcell, where I worked with many lawyers during my mediation work.

Rehana - I am grateful to The Straus Institute for Dispute Resolution at Pepperdine University for introducing me to Bill Eddy and Megan Hunter. It has been an amazing opportunity to work with HCI beyond my time at Pepperdine. And thank you to my mom, dad, and sister for extending grace and patience on this journey.

THE AUTHORS

Bill Eddy is a lawyer, therapist, mediator, and the co-founder and Chief Innovation Officer of the High Conflict Institute. He was the Senior Family Mediator at the National Conflict Resolution Center for fifteen years, a Certified Family Law Specialist lawyer representing clients in family court for fifteen years, and a therapist for twelve years. He serves on the faculty of the Straus Institute for Dispute Resolution at the Pepperdine University School of Law in California and is a Conjoint Associate Professor with the University of Newcastle Law School in Australia. He has been a speaker and trainer throughout the United States and around the world. He has written more than twenty books, including two award winners, is the co-host of the podcast *It's All Your Fault* and has a popular blog with Psychology Today with millions of views. Bill lives in San Diego, California with his wife.

Rehana Jamal is a conflict resolution specialist, mediator, and lawyer. She has always been fascinated by the way in which people interact, particularly in the way they communicate and navigate difficult conversations. This led her to pursue an undergraduate degree in psychology and, thereafter, a career in law and conflict resolution. Part of her work is to create and implement conflict resolution programs in schools and help reimagine a world where communities integrate conflict resolution as a guiding principle. Rehana holds an LL.M. in dispute resolution from Pepperdine Law School, a J.D. from Cardozo School of Law, and is a member of the New York State Bar. Her B.A. is in psychology from Barnard College, Columbia University. She has tremendous experience and passion working with people from different cultural, sociopolitical, and economic backgrounds.

9 781950 057399